SECOND ITERATION

MILLION MUSKMELONS

How to be like Elon Musk with Success Recipe for
Entrepreneurs and Leaders

PARAG MAHAJAN, MD

MedMantra, LLC
New Mexico

Second Edition of "MILLION MUSKMELONS: How to be like Elon Musk with Success Recipe for Entrepreneurs and Leaders" by Parag Mahajan, MD

Published by MedMantra, LLC

1330 San Pedro Drive NE STE 205A, Albuquerque, NM 87110

https://MedMantra.com

ISBN: 978-1-954612-00-6 (Paperback)

ISBN: 978-1-954612-01-3 (eBook)

Library of Congress Control Number: 2021930710 | Permalink: https://lccn.loc.gov/2021930710

Disclosure:

Parag Mahajan, the author, owns shares of and is bullish on Tesla (NASDAQ: TSLA)

Register your copy:

First edition: June 2019 | Second edition: February 2021

Register your copy of this book by following the instructions mentioned at https://MedMantra.com/mm

Registration entitles you to a completely free eBook of the next edition.

Speaker invitations and business consultation requests:

Contact the author by email (DrParag@MedMantra.com) for speaker invitations or business consultation requests.

DEDICATION

Nobody has been more important to me in the pursuit of writing this book than the members of my family. I would like to thank my parents, whose love and encouragement are with me in whatever I pursue. I would especially like to mention the forever cheerful attitude of my father, who maintained it even while being treated for stomach cancer recently. Most importantly, I wish to thank my loving and supportive wife, Anuradha, and my two wonderful daughters, Anoushka and Paavni, who provide unending inspiration. I would also like to thank my role models Elon Musk and Stephen Hawking, who inspired me to delve into the quest of the unknown.

Claim Your Surprise Gift

Thank you for checking out my book. To show my appreciation, I've prepared a special gift for all my readers that will help you master all the success principles of Elon Musk. The gift is in the form of regularly updated and free bonus articles, videos, training courses, and lots more.

Access it by visiting: **https://medmantra.com/mm**

TABLE OF CONTENTS

SECTION 1
A MILLION MUSKMELONS

CHAPTER ONE

WHAT ARE MUSKMELONS?

Introduction

There's no one quite like Elon Musk.

Whether you are just learning of the engineering genius and his extensive achievements or consider yourself one of his number one fans, you know the above statement to be true. Over the past two decades, the genius entrepreneur has positioned himself as one of the most dominant figures in the second technological revolution, as well as a cultural icon with the power to reshape humanity.

From PayPal to SpaceX, Elon Musk continues to reimagine the world we live in and play a defining role in the future of humanity. With so many achievements in the books, it's hard to imagine Musk—who has become the world's richest person—as anything other than a gigantic success.

Still, it's important to note that Musk, like the rest of us, started out small. As a child in Pretoria, South Africa, a young Elon Musk likely could not imagine his future success and riches. Born to an upper-middle-class family, Musk faced extreme loneliness at home and constant bullying at school.

How the genius was able to rise from such dire circumstances to become one of the world's most important men is one of the greatest stories of our lifetimes. For this reason, I wish to take a more detailed look at the several components that factored into his meteoric rise and examine what it is that makes Musk so special.

In doing so, I hope to lay out a blueprint for the rest of us. Namely, what qualities define what it means to be an "Elon Musk clone?" Answering this question can help the rest of us follow in Musk's footsteps—ultimately making the world a better place for all.

With enough resources in the universe to sustain a human population more than a million times what exists today, it's crucial that we understand how to inspire more Elon Musks to truly maximize our potential as a human race and make the world—and potentially the galaxy—a safer and smarter place for humanity.

With this in mind, let's jump into the meat of the matter and see exactly what it takes to be like Elon Musk.

Overview

Let's start with the most important question, "What is a muskmelon?"

In order to answer this, it's probably best to turn to my seven-year-old daughter. It *is* her term, after all. For the last three years, she and I have grown into the biggest Elon Musk fans on the planet. We love watching the genius entrepreneur revolutionize the tech industry, and we're excited about our own future trip to Mars.

One day, as we were discussing Musk, my daughter referred to him as "Muskmelon." The name, which was cute at first, ended up sticking, and now I imagine a different future for it. To me, a muskmelon is anyone who, like Elon Musk, learns to break the conventions of our time and revolutionize the world as we know it through hard work, technological innovation, and a desire to help all of humanity. In other words, **a muskmelon is an individualized Elon Musk "clone" who has all his good traits and follows in his footsteps to fundamentally change the way society operates and views the world.**

Obviously, these people are few and far between. With my daughter, I pondered why this is. Namely, why does it seem like individuals such as Musk come around only once in a generation? What we found out was that the answer was simpler than one may initially think.

The truth of the matter is that there are several "ingredients" to forming a proper muskmelon. For this reason, it's important that we take a look at what exactly makes up a muskmelon's DNA.

What Does It Take to Make a Muskmelon?

Surprisingly, many people get the wrong idea. One of the most popular misconceptions I see is that in order to be like Elon Musk, one must have a high IQ. According to these individuals, the entrepreneur's success has been built mostly (or even solely) on the back of his high IQ.

Based on this logic, most of us could never even hope to become muskmelons.

Fortunately, I'm here to say that this couldn't be further from the truth. While it's true that Musk possesses superior intelligence, it's simply wrong to say that his success can be boiled down to IQ.

If that were the case, we'd have more muskmelons already. Just think about it: there are countless individuals in the world with IQ levels similar to Musk's—but we never hear about them. Certainly, they aren't helping us get to Mars or revolutionizing our auto industries.

Based off this evidence alone, it's safe to say that it takes much more to be a muskmelon than simple intelligence. In this section, I'll go over some of the biggest traits that go into making a muskmelon. As you'll find, there are several important variables that go into being like Elon Musk—but with hard work and the right mindset, you can follow in the genius's footsteps.

- **Drive**

  When my daughter and I considered the qualities that make Elon Musk so special, the first idea we touched on was that of "drive." This concept is seen in everything that he does, and it's come to epitomize his work effort over the last few decades.

But what exactly do I mean when I say "drive"? It's actually pretty simple. Drive refers to the never-ending energy that Musk brings to his work. Elon is said to work between 70-100 hours per week.

Obviously, that's at least double the amount of time that the average individual works. Without this dedication, it's likely that Musk's Tesla would never have become a record-breaking electric car manufacturer by 2018.

Certainly, the genius's SpaceX program wouldn't have emerged into the world's leading private space program. The point here is this: it's impossible to become a muskmelon without drive. Anyone who's ever spent any time watching or researching him knows that Musk simply never stops moving.

Whether this means dropping by on his several projects—from Tesla to Neuralink—or appearing at tech conferences, Musk is always on the go. In fact, it can seem quite daunting just how much the entrepreneur is able to accomplish. We tend to think of Musk as a genius inventor and technological innovator, but the truth of the matter is that he is also a popular online personality (appearing in some of YouTube's most popular videos) and cultural icon who dominates both the Twittersphere and the online tech community.

How can one person come to prominence in so many fields? The answer is simple: drive. For aspiring muskmelons all across the world, this means that it's time to start injecting more energy into all your tasks. By bringing more awareness and drive to your activities, you'll be one step closer to achieving that coveted status for yourself.

- **Self-Belief**

How many times have you refrained from doing something just because you believed you couldn't do it? Better yet, how many times have you quit doing something you were passionate about because you didn't believe that you had the skills to complete it?

If you've ever experienced either one of these situations, it's likely that you suffer from poor self-belief. Not surprisingly, this stands in direct opposition to the qualities of a muskmelon.

Simply put, muskmelons possess strong self-belief and confidence that what they are doing is both right and feasible. Let's consider Elon Musk. Without a doubt, the engineering genius is the picture of self-belief. In fact, it's safe to say that self-confidence is the Tesla and SpaceX founder's most striking quality.

Think about it this way: how many people are willing to drop out of a Stanford PhD program to pursue their dreams? How many individuals would put over half their net worth into a risky business venture—which is exactly what Musk did with X.com?

The answer is, "Not many." As you can see, self-belief isn't just a feel-good motto for Elon Musk—it's a central part of who he is.

This means that self-belief is a key determining factor of what makes a muskmelon. Without belief in yourself—without the conviction that what you are doing can work—you will never be able to succeed in your ventures. For this reason, the wannabe muskmelons are asked to follow in Musk's footsteps. This means having the confidence to do what you desire with positive energy and the drive to succeed.

- **Perseverance**

When we look at Elon Musk, we tend to think of him as he is now: a very brilliant entrepreneur, cultural figure, and genius innovator. Despite this, it's crucial that we understand that he had humbler origins. While it's difficult for us to imagine Musk as anything other than a giant success, the truth of the matter is that Musk has had his own shares of ups and downs—just like the rest of us.

Take, for instance, his ousting from X.com. The company, which Musk formed in 1999 with $12 million of his own money, would eventually grow into the amazing PayPal service we know today. Musk, the company's original CEO, however, was not always considered a popular figure. Though he oversaw the company's merger with rival Confinity—who initially thought of and implemented PayPal—and grew the business into a large-scale corporation with hundreds of employees—many of his workers lacked confidence in him as a leader.

As a result, Musk was ousted from his role as CEO during a vacation to Africa. The ousting, which marked Musk's most crushing defeat, effectively ended Musk's control of his own company X.com, which would be sold to eBay just a few years later.

Despite this, Musk remained undeterred. Though he lost his position and the confidence of many partners and employees, Musk continued to invest in PayPal and helped grow it into the service we recognize today. More importantly, however, he did not let his defeat get him down. Instead, he used his own capital again to form another business—this one even more ambitious than the former.

This business, which Musk named SpaceX, currently dominates private space travel and enterprise. Without a spirit of perseverance, it's likely that Musk would never have been able to rebuild himself from defeat and go on to bigger and bolder challenges.

Since his ousting from X.com, Musk has also cemented himself as one of the most dominant figures in the auto industry. What's more, he's earned another CEO position—this time of innovative and world-leading Tesla, Inc., which Musk helped grow from infancy.

The message here is clear: it's impossible to become a muskmelon without the ability to recover from failure. Just as perseverance is a key part of who Elon Musk is, it should also be a central component of anyone who wishes to follow in the entrepreneur's footsteps.

- **Desire to Help Humanity**

What attracts my daughter and me most to Elon Musk isn't his success nor his financial achievements. While these qualifications are no doubt impressive, what most draws us to Elon is his desire to help humanity. From revolutionizing the banking industry with PayPal to drafting plans to colonize Mars, Musk is all about making the human experience more enjoyable and more sustainable.

This can perhaps best be seen in his work with Tesla. Though Musk started out only as an investor and chairman to the company, he quickly gained the CEO position and has helped make Tesla the world's leading electric car manufacturer.

Importantly, it's not profits that drive Musk to create better and more innovative electric car technology. Rather, it's a desire to make human energy consumption more sustainable, more affordable, and better for the planet at large. With electric cars, Musk believes we can cut down on the consumption of fossil fuels and save the environment for generations to come.

That's part of the reason Musk has merged his incredible Tesla with the nation's leading solar energy business—SolarCity. Through the introduction of solar batteries and other technology to the Tesla brand, Musk hopes to make solar energy more affordable and functional worldwide.

For the muskmelon, this means that having a desire to help humanity is a crucial aspect to following in Musk's footsteps. Being a muskmelon requires that individuals have a plan to make the world a better place for all of humanity.

This means that compassion, ingenuity, and an unending desire to help others are all indispensable for those wishing to become the next Elon Musk.

- **Creativity**

What is it that truly sets Elon Musk apart, however? There are several individuals with the above qualities who aren't building rocket ships, after all. While the above qualities can be considered necessary ingredients to becoming a muskmelon, no one can follow after the engineering genius without a bit of creativity.

We also call this innovation. One of the defining aspects of Musk's career is his ability to consistently think outside the box. Simply put, what other entrepreneurs call impossible, the entrepreneur calls easy.

This is why we've seen Musk send astronauts to the International Space Station. It's also why we're currently witnessing history as the genius entrepreneur takes concrete steps to reach Mars as early as 2024.

Perhaps no matter demonstrates Musk's innovation quite as clearly as the Hyperloop, however. The project, which would see passengers transported by trains in a vacuum tube, would allow humans to reach their destinations at the speed of sound.

While this may sound like science fiction to most, Musk has already taken several steps to make this a reality. In fact, the first Hyperloop "pods" are already under construction. From this example, it's clear that being a "muskmelon" takes more than simply working hard or for a good purpose.

Muskmelons must be able to think outside the box. This innovation is necessary for revolutionizing the human experience and creating a world that's not only different but better than the one we inhabit today.

What This Means for Us

With all this being said, you may be thinking, "What does this mean for us?"

Luckily, I have the answer to that. Now that we know what qualities go into making a muskmelon, it is our responsibility to follow through with the next step. This means that we should embody these qualities in ourselves and help others find them as well.

As I talked about this with my daughter, she posed an interesting question, "What would the world be like with a million muskmelons?"

The question, which at first seemed difficult to answer, played over and over in my mind. In the end, I decided that the question—which was posed innocently by a seven-year-old—has significant real-world merit.

Think about it this way: with one Elon Musk doing so much for the world, what miracles could we expect to experience if at least one million others adopted Musk's model and took up the torch to make the universe a better place?

In the next chapter, we will examine the important implications that having one million muskmelons could have for the world. In doing so, we will examine in more detail Musk's incredible impact on our society and what we can do to become more like him.

Elon Musk Offered Permanent Residency in China

In 2019, China offered permanent residency to the Tesla CEO, Elon Musk. This step was taken in response to the substantial presence that the car-manufacturing company Tesla has established in China.

Musk visited the Land of Dragons for the groundbreaking ceremony of the Tesla Gigafactory in Shanghai in January 2019. With this, Shanghai became Tesla's first production base outside the US. Two days after this announcement, Musk met with Chinese premier Li Keqiang to discuss the future plans of the business. This big move by Musk was appreciated by Li because it could be considered the starting point of a larger global trade. The speed of decision-making and the execution abilities of Musk could be witnessed through the fact that the construction of this project began just three months after he booked a piece of land in the Industrial zone in Lingang.

The founder of America's best-selling electric car company is in love with China. He confirmed this during the meeting with Li Keqiang and presented his wish to visit there more often. Li's reply to this came as a welcoming gesture, offering Musk a "Chinese Green Card."

With the goal of setting Tesla's Shanghai factory as a global example, Tesla is looking forward to increasing its empire in the Peoples' Republic of China. However, it must be noted that getting a green card in China is not as easy as it is in the United States. In terms of numbers, the US gave permanent residency to more than a million people in 2017. On the other hand, the number of foreign nationals with Chinese permanent residency was noted to be around 10,000 in 2016. Very few privileged people, like Nobel-prize-winning economist Robert Mundell, former NBA champion Stephon Marbury, Nobel-award-winning chemistry scientist Bernard Feringa, and a few more have received the rare opportunity to get China's green card.

Tesla plans to produce cost-effective variants of its famous Model 3 and Model Y cars in this recently created Gigafactory base in China and has the aim of growing quickly in its production. Seeing this as a bigger opportunity, China has offered Musk permanent residency in China. However, it is worth waiting for Musk's response, as the genius entrepreneur has not yet commented on this through his Twitter handle, where otherwise he is actively engaged.

CHAPTER TWO

IS IT POSSIBLE TO FIND A MILLION MUSKMELONS?

Elon "Muskmelon's" innovations are changing the face of technology today. From the commercialization of space travel to the development of state-of-the-art electric vehicles, the entrepreneur's ambition has earned him respect across the world.

My daughter and I have long admired Musk's never-ending drive—and we've noticed one thing. Musk's resume and a long list of accomplishments look like they're the result of multiple people. It got us to thinking, "how can one man accomplish so much?"

Even more interesting: what would the world look like if there were a million muskmelons? If we could find a million people with this kind of hyper-productivity, we'd likely be living in a world that we didn't recognize. We might actually be able to achieve the futuristic visions outlined in nearly every science fiction novel. We'd be in a world completely revolutionized by technology.

We'd be on an accelerated path to greatness.

I can guess what you're thinking.

"Musk is an exceptional genius." "There will never be another Elon Musk—at least not in our lifetimes."

While these thoughts are understandable, what if I told you that they're wrong? In fact, they're not just wrong: they're damaging.

By viewing the possibility of having a million muskmelons as something obtainable, we can get on the right track to maximizing human potential.

But is it possible to have a million muskmelons? Is that a reasonable goal to which we should aspire?

The answer is yes—and it's on us, all of us, to make sure that we're developing the talent today that we'll need for tomorrow.

That being said, let's take a look at what the world would look like with a million muskmelons—and just what it will take to get us there.

What Would a World with a Million Muskmelons Look Like?

My daughter and I had a fun time trying to answer this question. Trying to imagine the potential achievements we would reach with a million muskmelons can be quite exciting—and it requires having a large amount of creativity.

We'll take a look at how we see the world playing out if we had a million muskmelons. But first, take a moment to imagine for yourself. Don't let us have all the fun! Once you've had enough imagining, consider the following ways that we see the world changing if there were a million muskmelons:

1. The World Would Be Bigger

First and foremost, if the world had a million muskmelons, it would grow. Exponentially.

Why do we know that?

Just consider the ways that Musk has already worked to reduce the size of the world—and our universe. Through his ambitions to make commercialized space travel possible, Musk has made it his mission to make space living and exploration a reality.

While working for this, his company SpaceX has become the first private organization in the world to launch a crewed orbital spacecraft (Crew Dragon Demo 2) in May 2020. It was also the first private company to be approved by NASA to man certain missions to space. And the list of achievements doesn't stop there. From the development of reusable rockets to manning crews to the International Space Station, Musk has been leading innovations in the field of space travel.

It's something that he hopes will make the human colonization of Mars a possibility during our lifetimes.

This ambitious project comes from the mind of the one-and-only Elon Musk. But what if there were a million muskmelons all working to achieve the same goal?

Not only would it be accomplished sooner, but it would likely be accomplished through the development of new technology that had other powerful implications. Even more importantly, the goal would likely expand. Instead of wanting to colonize Mars, a million muskmelons would want to go after the entire solar system and then the next. With a million muskmelons working toward this goal, you can be sure that the end result would be one that the rest of us could only dream about.

2. We'd Take Better Care of Our World

Elon Musk has been an eco-friendly trailblazer for a number of years. The work he has done with the development of state-of-the-art electric cars has revitalized what some experts had called a dead industry.

With electric cars now becoming more affordable and easier to purchase under Musk, it's key to note just how far we've come. From gas-guzzlers to new electric vehicles, citizens are beginning to shift away from traditional forms of transportation.

Musk's Tesla company has played a large role in this, helping to redefine how we view electric cars.

However great this has been, we can only imagine how much better it would have been with a million muskmelons. With a million people working at hyper levels of productivity in order to protect our environment, we can be sure that our world would be much better taken care of.

Now, Musk has been largely focused on helping the environment through the development of new electric cars. If there were a million muskmelons, we could be sure that they would find a million other ways to protect the environment.

This would lead to new eco-friendly practices that upgrade our societies and help protect our planet. In this way, humans would be able to reduce our carbon footprint while still advancing our societies. In other words, we could stop taking a toll on the planet and other inhabitants living here just so that we could advance.

This futuristic vision still feels far away from our current policies and practices. However, as Musk has already proven to be true, these expectations can be shattered through the hard work of one individual.

Now, if we could manage to develop a growing number of muskmelons to combat other environmental problems, we could establish quite possibly the greatest plan to combat climate change to ever exist.

3. Transportation Would Be at the Speed of Sound

Elon Musk's work to revolutionize transportation doesn't stop at space travel or electric cars, however. The at-times eccentric genius has also worked to provide transportation to the populace at the speed of sound.

That's right—his work on a project known as the Hyperloop looks to make transportation much faster than anyone else currently thinks possible.

Though this project is still in its early stages, it looks to have a great effect on how we travel and get around. If it is one day realized—which we're sure it will—then the face of human transportation will be changed forever.

How would that change if we had a million muskmelons working to complete similar projects?

We can only imagine. With this many qualified individuals working on the problem, we're sure that our transportation would start to mirror something from a science fiction novel. And while we're not sure if we're willing to put teleportation on the list of things that could be accomplished, we wouldn't be all that surprised if it did.

4. Technology Would Work for Us

A common theme that can be found through Elon's work is that technology starts to work for us. All too often, we may think that there's not much that we can do with the technology that we have. Instead, we're limited by what innovations will or won't be possible—and then we have to learn to live with that.

Musk breaks through these traditional notions with some of the most revolutionary innovations that we have seen over the last two decades. His willingness to work on projects that others call impossible has helped him become one of the most successful and highly-respected innovators of our time.

With this in mind, one can confidently say that Musk looks to develop technology that works for us. By adopting his attitude that we're not passive in the face of technological change, we can start developing even more innovations that would change the way that we navigate the world.

If there were a million muskmelons, we could be especially sure that the new age of technology would become even more human friendly.

By this, I mean that we would have a technological revolution that would serve human interests—that's because more and more individuals would be inspired to create technology that before they could only dream about.

5. Humans Would Remain Dominant

Finally, if the world had a million muskmelons, humans would have no reason to fear that they were going to lose their place on the total pole any time soon.

Musk himself remains terrified at the possibility that soon artificial intelligence could catch up to humans. It's a situation that he cautions against, noting that if technology were able to develop on its own, it would no longer be concerned with advancing human interests.

This, of course, would become a problem, as humans may not have access to the superhuman intelligence that some machines can exhibit in some areas.

For this reason, Musk has worked to combat the rise of artificial intelligence with two companies of his own: Neuralink and Open AI. These two companies work to make sure that humans aren't powerless in the face of this rapid technological change.

How would this look if there were a million muskmelons? Let me count the ways:

First, it might be quite possible that humans would be able to compete with machine intelligence. Though not much is known about Musk's secretive AI developments, it has been reported that one of his companies, Neuralink, is developing implantable brain machine interfaces (BMIs). In July 2019, Neuralink announced that it was working on a "sewing machine-like" device capable of implanting very thin electrode threads into the brain, with a human trial expected to begin in late 2020. In August 2020, Neuralink demonstrated a functional surgical robot designed to insert a FitBit like coin-shaped device (the N1 implant/sensor) in the skull and to insert the neural threads/electrodes safely into the brain. Neuralink received a Breakthrough Device designation from the Food and Drug Administration (FDA) in July 2020. After successful implantations in pigs, the startup is now preparing for its first human implantation, pending required approvals and further safety testing. Neuralink's ultimate goal is to give us access to the same thinking that AI systems will have.

These interesting bits of news suggest that if there were a million muskmelons, humans would be able to develop in a way that we have never quite done before.

On a broader scale, however, the change would be even more different. Instead of developing AI systems that even have the threat of becoming so advanced, we could be sure that researchers would create technology to help us—and not replace us.

Now that we've looked at the ways that the world would differ with a million muskmelons, it's time to answer the question you've all been waiting for.

Is it even possible to find a million muskmelons?

The answer is, of course, yes—so let me show you how.

Is It Possible to Find a Million Muskmelons?

The answer may not be quite so straightforward as you would think. That's because you don't really just "find" a muskmelon. Instead, we have a responsibility to make sure that we're developing muskmelons.

Develop a Million Muskmelons

What does this mean?

For one, we have to realize that a certain number of amazing circumstances must come into play if you are looking to find a muskmelon. Remember that Elon Musk was not created overnight. A long series of events throughout his life have made it so that he believes in his dreams and works to make them come true.

These are not qualities that most people lack. In fact, as children, we're all quite similar to Elon Musk. However, at that age, we're quite powerless to make our dreams come true in the world. Instead, our goals at that time should be to make sure that we're maintaining the right attitudes to make achieving our goals later a possibility.

But how can we do that as children? As a father with a young daughter, let me tell you: we can't. Instead, our goal should be to make sure that we're fostering the right environment for our children to grow in positive ways.

All of this must first start, however, by making sure that we're appropriately developing ourselves. No matter what our situations are, with a little self-care, we can start turning ourselves into muskmelons.

Below, I'll walk you through the important characteristics we must maintain for ourselves and grow in our children if we ever want to see a world with a million muskmelons.

For Ourselves

As noted, in order to help others develop their own inner muskmelons, we should first work on ourselves. To do this, we must live by what I call the "3 A's." These three characteristics are what we need to maintain to develop into muskmelons on our own.

- **Accountability**

The first trait that we should take from Musk is accountability. This means that we recognize that our actions have consequences—and then we act accordingly.

As Musk shows, one of the biggest crimes that we can do is *not acting*. This can occur for a variety of reasons—from laziness to fear. Addressing the underlying cause of our inability to take action can help us reach the levels of productivity required to become muskmelons on our own.

- **Ambition**

Next, if we want to become muskmelons, we need to make sure that we never lose our ambition. This means not giving up on our dreams no matter how impossible they seem—and no matter what anyone else says.

It can be difficult to be ambitious when it appears that life better rewards practicality. However, make sure that you don't get so caught up in the day-to-day burdens of life that you forget to live.

By keeping our ambitions close to heart and taking action to work on them, we can start to be muskmelons on our own.

- **Answers**

Finally, to become muskmelons, we're going to have to make sure that we always look for the answers.

Even the hard ones.

This means that when life throws something our way, we don't back away because it's inconvenient. Instead, we work to find the answers so that we can better navigate through life. By doing so, we'll also further our own abilities, as well as our drive. Ultimately, this allows us to get more of what we need to get done, done.

For Our Kids

Don't forget that one of the best ways to make a million muskmelons is to develop them throughout life. Best of all, by doing this, we can provide a better life for our children. This is because the number of little muskmelons we can create is unlimited.

To do this, we must teach our children the "3 S's." Check these three traits out below!

- **Self-Esteem**

   One of the most important things that we can teach our children is self-esteem. This is done in a variety of ways.

   For instance, make sure that you're teaching your child the importance of self-esteem while fostering an environment in which they feel comfortable. Encourage them to do more and to do their best—over time; they'll develop the confidence they need to go after their dreams like true muskmelons.

- **Sincerity**

   Next, we'll need to make sure that we teach our children that money isn't the most important thing to go after. Instead, they'll need to be sincere in their ambitions to help others and to help the planet.

   This mindset comes straight from Musk—whose ambitious deals have worked to change the world for the better. By instilling this value in our children from a young age, we can make sure they stay more focused and dedicated to their goals.

- **Synergy**

   Finally, we need to make sure that our children understand the value of synergy. By being able to work well with each other and learn from each other's ideas, children can develop the skills it truly takes to become muskmelons.

With this in mind, remember, there's no better time than now to start developing the muskmelons in ourselves and in our children.

Through a little hard work, we can make the goal of a million muskmelons a reality sooner than we ever thought possible.

Elon Musk Started a School for His Kids!

Did you know that the famous Tesla star Elon Musk has started a school for his kids? Yes, you heard that right! He sincerely believes that every child has different interests, aptitudes, and abilities that should be nurtured during their education. Another fundamental concept that he abides by is the art of problem-solving. According to him, kids should be taught problem-solving rather than tools for problem-solving. This way, they learn the application of knowledge gained and, thus, the relevance of the tools. For example, if you want them to learn about a screwdriver, don't teach a course on the parts of the screwdriver and its uses. Rather, just introduce them to machines, ask them to open something, and when they don't know how to do that, show them the screwdriver. Let them know that a screwdriver is just a tool, while the main focus is on solving the problem.

When he found no school practicing these principles, he decided to create a separate little school for his kids to learn. He began a small school with 14 kids and named it Ad Astra, which means "to the stars." He envisioned this school as being different from most of the regular schools, in order to make the process of learning enjoyable. Instead of differentiating kids based on grades like Grade 1, Grade 2, Grade 3, etc., this school keeps them all in the same grade. Furthermore, this school has an amazing admissions strategy, in which students can select from a number of options based on their thinking and reasoning skills. The culture of the school welcomes children from various backgrounds, but they don't pay the same amount of fees to get admitted. Instead, the school has a variable tuition fee system depending on the income and wealth of the household that the child comes from and also their parents' paying capacities.

Can you believe that Elon Musk hated going to school right from his childhood? School seemed to be torturous to him. Throughout years of experience, he became convinced that schools and colleges are not for learning; they're just another part of one's daily routine, mainly to spend some time with one's friends. Additionally, stale homework assignments make it obvious that conventional education systems do nothing but download data into students' brains instead of developing a significant thinking process. Learning, according to Elon Musk, does not happen when there is a lack of enthusiasm. If professors in college keep teaching the same old thing in the same repeated way for many years without questioning if it is relevant today, how do you expect students to be excited about it? On the other hand, if students are directed to explore "why" in their learning, they understand the basic purpose of it and feel motivated.

Do you still think that it is necessary to go to college to be successful? If you follow Elon Musk, you must know that graduating with a good degree from a good college might help you master some subjects, but that is not the only way to be successful. Musk appreciates people like Gates, Jobs, and Ellison, who were smart as well as courageous enough to leave college and start something new. They believed in something and chased it with their unique and original talent, which Musk calls, "Exceptional Ability."

Musk is so sure about his thoughts on formal education that he has created an unusual hiring criterion at his company. When selecting a person as an employee, Musk is not interested in knowing his/her degree or education. In fact, he interviews the person to get an idea of how he/she has managed to face difficult times in life and how he/she has taken a stand at turning points. That's sufficient for him to get an instinct about that person. Musk has faith that when someone is going through a tough situation, he/she is thoroughly aware of the real struggles confronted in the process. If someone pretends to have done something but has not actually done it, he/she will certainly not have an answer to questions on further details. On the other hand, a truthful person doesn't fail to answer even the minute points genuinely. Elon Musk can sense from their answer whether that person was actually responsible for rising above the adversity. It is then evident if that person has really used his/her exceptional ability to accomplish something significant.

That means, even if you have never gone to a high school but can prove that your mind works with an exceptional ability to solve problems, keep going, as you are on the right track!

CHAPTER THREE

WHY THE WORLD NEEDS A MILLION ELON MUSKS?

Introduction

It's likely that we won't see another Elon Musk in our lifetimes.

The genius electric car maker and SpaceX chief engineer plays a dominant role in today's culture and seemingly shapes the future of the world with each new action. With several high-profile and game-changing companies under his belt—of which Tesla and SpaceX are just a few—Musk is among a select group of peers when it comes to power and influence.

Still, it's fun to imagine what the world would be like if we had more than one Elon Musk. Already, we've seen Elon raise the electric car industry from the dead and revitalize the United States' space program.

What, then, would life be like if we had a million Elon Musks? That's the question we'll try to answer in this chapter. Let's take a look at each one of Musk's significant contributions and goals and see what it would be like if we had a world of people dedicated to them with the same passion and fervor.

Ready? Let's begin!

The Basics

A few things are clear. First, Elon Musk deserves to be called one of the greatest visionaries of our time. From revitalizing space travel to helping cut back on the world's pollution, Musk leads the way in the private scientific revolution. Currently, his actions pave the way for this age's technological revolution. The engineering genius plays a significant role in the development of modern society.

How is Elon Musk changing the world? Let's see a brief overview of his current accomplishments:

- Helped start PayPal, the world's most popular digital currency processor

- Commercialized electric cars

- Popularized solar energy

- Brought back US space travel

This list serves only as a sample of what Musk has already accomplished for the world. The best part? Musk isn't even halfway done, with his future plans even more daring and adventurous than his current accomplishments.

With this in mind, let's take a look at a few ways having a million Elon Musks could benefit all of mankind—and change the world.

How Could One Million Elon Musks Help the World?

1. Revolutionize Currency

Before Elon Musk's involvement in PayPal, there was no online digital payment system. Though the genius entrepreneur did not found PayPal, which actually started as a rival service that came under his domain with the X.com-Confinity merger in 2000, he did play a large role in its development as the world's foremost digital transaction service. In fact, Musk remained a large shareholder in PayPal for years—even after his ousting from the company.

With a wide-open cryptocurrency market, it becomes interesting to hypothesize what a million Elon Musks could do for the world. With national currencies tied so heavily to federal regulations and national banks, there's been a push to popularize cryptocurrencies. This push mirrors Musk's own push from nearly two decades ago to have an online digital currency system that could handle Internet transactions.

A million Elon Musks could change the future of currency and revolutionize the way we view poverty and wealth. With people no longer being tied down to traditional forms of currency, wealth would be a loose concept more accessible to people from all across the world—even in developing nations.

Musk himself has this to say about cryptocurrency: "It bypasses currency controls... Paper money is going away. And crypto is a far better way to transfer values than a piece of paper, that's for sure."

The genius engineer lamented the current "energy-intensive" nature of cryptocurrencies such as Bitcoin, which he states is counter to the sustainable-energy goals of his companies. Still, it seems that Musk is all in for the idea of cryptocurrencies.

While the idea may not be feasible yet, with one million Elon Musks, the new-age currency revolution could have a major impact on the way we view money, wealth, and poverty.

What's for sure is that Musk has already changed the trajectory of currency by helping introduce one of the world's first and most successful digital currency options. Knowing this, who can say what impact one million such individuals would have on the world?

2. Develop E-Commerce

Musk's involvement in PayPal proved revolutionary in another way: through this digital currency, mankind finally had a reliable way to venture into e-commerce. Though most of us couldn't imagine a world without commerce giants such as Amazon or eBay, these online stores owe a lot of their worth to payment systems such as PayPal that spurred the growth of the digital currency.

Without a doubt, e-commerce has forever changed the way consumers shop. Individuals are no longer bound to traditional brick-and-mortar stores in their current geographical location. Instead, it's possible to buy goods from across the world. Just as importantly, it's now possible for consumers to pay for goods without accessing their bank accounts.

Specifically, many physical locations have begun to accept PayPal and other forms of digital currency as viable payment options. This means that the consumer is no longer tied to traditional payment options such as credit, debit, or cash—giving the consumer more freedom and control over his finances. Still, e-commerce is an imperfect system, with high shipping rates and oftentimes confusing currency conversions.

Imagine, then, what a million Elon Musk-esque entrepreneurs could do to further revolutionize e-commerce. With the development of better payment systems and greater access to online shops, consumers could have a world of unlimited goods at their fingertips.

Entrepreneurs like Elon Musk are spurring a digital revolution like never seen before. This vision—which would bring ultimate convenience to the consumer—could be completed through the actions of several entrepreneurs who share the same vision and energy as Musk.

3. Commercialize Renewable Energy

In order to hypothesize what a million Elon Musks could do for the world, let's take a look at what the Founder, CEO, and Lead Designer of SpaceX has already done for renewable energy. Currently, Musk serves as CEO of SolarCity, a company he helped found in 2006 with his cousins Peter and Lyndon Rive.

What has the company been able to accomplish since? Quite a lot, as it turns out. Though Musk remained largely hands-off until the acquisition of SolarCity by Tesla in 2016, by 2013, SolarCity had established itself as the leading residential solar energy installer in the United States—and the number two overall installer of solar energy. In the company's heyday, they were installing nearly 30% of residential solar energy across the United States per year.

Since Tesla's acquisition of SolarCity in 2016, Musk has endeavored to make SolarCity a valuable part of the Tesla brand. In fact, SolarCity plays a large role in the development of Tesla's solar panels, roofing materials, batteries, and other products. In Musk's own words, the SolarCity acquisition was designed to make Tesla a completely "clean" company—meaning that the company uses only renewable energy.

In doing so, Musk could help millions of people across the world begin to live lower-energy lifestyles. As Tesla currently sits at the top of the electric car business—and as Musk continually defines himself as a cultural icon of the current generation—the value of Tesla's clean energy policy cannot be understated. Already, one Elon Musk is shaping the world in a positive direction when it comes to renewable energy. In fact, if Tesla gets its way, the world may experience a sort of energy revolution in the coming years.

Knowing this, what could a million Elon Musks do? For starters, if more business owners were like Elon Musk, the switch to renewable energy would have been made long ago. With a majority of business owners holding out on updating their energy policies—especially in developing nations—it's clear that the commercialization of renewable energy has a long way to go.

With a million Elon Musks, there would be a greater push for renewable energy and more innovation in making it possible. Already, the genius has secured plans to make Tesla the world's first completely clean automobile company.

And that's without sacrificing any of the car's quality or any of the company's value.

That's a pretty impressive feat, and it's one that, if replicated, could seriously change the world and the way we view energy. Think about it this way: what if feats such as the ones Tesla routinely pulls off weren't considered groundbreaking as they are now? What if they were simply normal because the world was full of people like Elon Musk?

One thing is clear: if that were the case, the world would be a much better place. Still, as the genius entrepreneur continues to knock down barriers and set lofty goals for himself and for his company, it's likely that the path to commercializing renewable energy will only become clearer in the coming years. Perhaps this will be the push the world needs to develop more individuals with the same dedication to saving the planet through a focus on clean, renewable energy that—in the long run, anyway—will be much cheaper for the consumers and bodes better for the environment.

4. Decrease Pollution

This leads us to our next point. As of 2017, Tesla claimed to have saved the world from 2.5 million tons of carbon emissions.

Let that sink in for a minute.

That's 2.5 million tons of toxic fumes that will never be released into the environment, weakening our planet and contributing to global warming. If you don't think that's a big deal, think again. This statistic only becomes more impressive when you realize that Tesla is still in its beginning stages. Of course, the company isn't new— that's not the claim.

But there's no denying that, with advancements in technology and Musk's continuous ingenuity, the company has a long way to go. In fact, Musk dreams of a world with completely electric vehicles—and interesting transportation systems for them to participate in. If the engineering genius has his way, it's likely that gasoline-powered vehicles will disappear from the picture altogether.

And how great would that be? While most of us love our gas-guzzlers, there's no denying that they are harmful to the environment. Not only do they contribute to air pollution, but they also bring about a few emissions-related deaths per year—a risk that doesn't exist with electric vehicles.

When Musk started at Tesla Motors, there was no dominant electric vehicle in the United States—or in the world. In fact, after the failure of GM's EV1—the company's landmark vehicle that was supposed to put them in the market for electric automobiles—many outlets reported that the electric car industry was dead.

It only makes sense, then, that it would take an innovator like Musk to revive the industry and take it to new heights. In 2018, Tesla, Inc. became the largest and best-selling manufacturer of electric vehicles— and it wasn't even close. With several consumers around the world making the switch to electric—and what Musk hopes will soon become completely "clean" electric—the genius is helping save the world from carbon pollution, one consumer at a time.

What's more, as Tesla continues to expand into international markets (with vehicles on the road in at least thirty-seven different nations), it's clear that the company is having an impact in more than just the first-world.

What if, however, there were more than one Elon Musk? What if, perhaps, there were a million? A million minds committed to one goal: the end of environmentally-damaging pollution.

With a million Elon Musks, developing countries, as well, could have access to clean energy and enjoy low levels of pollution. Standards of living across the world would soar as air quality improves.

As the Earth continues to suffer from global warming, a phenomenon worsened daily by human pollution, it's crucial that like-minded entrepreneurs gather in the vein of Elon Musk and find ways to combat the current climate crisis.

5. Make Humans an Interplanetary Species

In some ways, a world full of Elon Musks would be like living in some of history's greatest science fiction novels.

For example, Musk's goal of interplanetary space travel proves a lofty, science-fiction-esque goal. That hasn't stopped him, however, from forming SpaceX.

SpaceX has become one of—if not the—most successful private space-travel companies in world history. The first private space rocket engineering company to put a reusable rocket into orbit and retrieve it, SpaceX looks to bring humans to Mars.

SpaceX serves as the vehicle of Musk's dreams to commercialize travel between Earth and Mars. The entrepreneur's company is currently working to develop technology that will make interplanetary travel possible.

Musk scored a win when SpaceX received certification from NASA to take both cargo and crews to the International Space Station. With the genius entrepreneur on the path to redefining space technology, one can't help but wonder: how far along would we be if the world had a million Elon Musks?

We can think of a few ways:

- **Mars Would Be the Hottest Vacation Spot**

That's right. We're confident that if the world had a million Elon Musks, commercialized travel to Mars would already exist.

Not only that, with Musk's latest designs providing for cheaper interplanetary space travel, we're also sure that it would be affordable. This means that going to Mars wouldn't be reserved for the rich elite.

Instead, it would be such a commonplace occurrence that Mars could literally be considered a vacation spot.

And let's be real: who would go to the beach when they could go to Mars?

- **Mars Might Be Livable**

Yep—if there were a million Elon Musks, it might be possible to do more than just take a trip to Mars.

It might even be possible to live there.

Even now, Musk has a goal of having 80,000 people on Mars by the year 2040—and the first people are expected to travel there in the early 2020s.

So how might this be possible?

Musk and his team, along with NASA, are also looking for signs of water on the planet and look to develop technology that would enable humans to live on Mars.

How's that for increasing the total amount of real estate?

And with a million Elon Musks, we're sure that it could happen. In fact, it's likely that this lofty goal would have occurred already.

Which leads us to think …

- **We'd Colonize the Solar System**

If one Elon Musk can take us to Mars and help us colonize it by 2040, a million would close the gap between all the planets in the solar system.

Instead of deciding what country to live in, you could decide which planet. Similar to the rush to colonize the New World in the 1500 and 1600s, there would be a mad scramble as countries looked to take over planets.

It's hard to imagine what a colonized solar system would look like. But what we do know is that if we had a million Elon Musks, traveling from one planet to the other would be similar to flying between countries today.

This game-changing technology would open a world of possibilities and take us straight into the *Twilight Zone*.

As you can see, having this many Elon Musks would do more than change the world. It'd change the very nature of the universe as we know it.

The only thing that we can't figure out is this: if the world had a million Elon Musks, what would be considered science fiction?

6. Reduce Traffic Accidents

What makes Elon Musk so special? Primarily the fact that his efforts don't just stop there. He is constantly thinking of ways to improve standards of living around the world. Take, for instance, his push for self-driving cars.

In early 2019, Musk remarked on his goal to have a fully-functioning self-driving Tesla car by the year 2020, "I think we will be feature-complete on full self-driving this year, meaning the car will be able to find you in a parking lot, pick you up, take you all the way to your destination without an intervention this year."

Those are some pretty bold words. While we'll have to wait to test it for ourselves, it's safe to say that we are living in exciting times. Through Musk's technology, we may soon reach the point where we can "snooze behind the wheel," as the entrepreneur put it. This would mean a significant reduction in traffic accidents and a whole new driving experience.

Let's put it this way: with technology that can avoid collisions and help drivers get to their destinations with minimal driver input, it's likely that automobile accidents will become a thing of the past. As of 2019, there are over six million car accidents a year, with more than ninety deaths per day.

Musk is seeking to change that. With the entrepreneur's self-driving technology, it's likely that this number will see a significant drop-off. In other words, Elon Musk is saving lives.

Still, Elon's efforts have been met with scorn from the greater technological community. Several manufacturers doubt his ability to have a fully-functioning self-driving vehicle.

What if the world had a million Elon Musks, however? What if the same people who deride the Tesla and SpaceX founder now would join the cause and work toward the development of true self-driving vehicles?

It's safe to say that Musk would reach his goal much faster. It's also safe to say that over the course of the next few decades, millions of lives would be saved from potentially-fatal automobile accidents. Because of this, the fully-functioning self-driving Tesla model that Musk is currently working on is one of his most important inventions yet.

As such, it's important not to just imagine what it would be like to have more than one Elon Musk. It's time to pick up the entrepreneur's mantle and join him in the crusade for safer and more reliable transportation.

7. Revolutionize Transportation

With projects such as the Hyperloop, the Boring Company, and self-driving cars, Elon Musk leads the pack in terms of the transportation revolution. Imagine how early Americans must have felt with the invention of the railroad and, later, Henry Ford's Model T.

Perhaps global citizens should feel the same way today. Musk, who is often referred to as a "real-life Tony Stark," claims to be on the cusp of revolutionary technological developments that could completely alter the way we view transportation.

Not only is the entrepreneur the leading producer of electric cars the world has ever seen, but he also dabbles in other projects that seek to change the face of transportation forever. Most notable among these endeavors is the point-to-point transport on Earth using Starship, which seeks to commercialize rocket transport on Earth to travel between any two cities at hypersonic speed in less than an hour. The other notable endeavor being the Hyperloop.

While it may sound like the science-fiction dream of an eccentric genius, Musk is committed to showing that the ideas can work in reality. The SpaceX Starship system is in development through rapid iterations at its Boca Chica, Texas facility. Already, miles of pipe for the Hyperloop has been laid, and development teams from MIT and other professional institutions have begun working on ways to make the Hyperloop a reality.

But it's not just speed-of-sound trains and hypersonic rockets that the genius is working on. With his Boring Company, which seeks to reduce the cost of tunnel boring by a factor of ten, Elon is paving the way for the future of automobile transportation. The goal? To dig safe underground tunnels that will allow self-driving cars to move along tracks. With these tunnels, Musk claims, we'll never have to worry about traffic again. This would speed up transportation and make it easier for individuals to get from Point A to Point B.

The best part? Not only would these goals revolutionize the safety and the convenience of transportation, but they would also help human transportation become "green." Because Musk is committed to 100% renewable and clean energy, these new projects would usher in an era of clean energy that would decrease humankind's carbon footprint and save the environment from future damage.

What does all this mean? It means that the effort and dreams of just one man can go a long way to shaping the world for billions of people. Knowing this, it's worth imagining what a million Elon Musks could do for transportation—and the world.

With a million Elon Musks, it's possible the world could experience the first true flying cars (though Musk himself isn't a huge fan of the idea). It's also possible that we develop vehicles that can move at hyperspeed—which Musk states the Hyperloop will eventually be able to do.

What's clear is that entrepreneurs must follow Musk's model in order to accelerate and facilitate positive change in the world.

8. Eradicate Poverty

Imagine a world with no poverty.

One of the toughest problems plaguing humanity, poverty, has evaded solutions for millennia. At best, people have worked to find ways to reduce its impact on a global and a local scale.

But if the world had a million Elon Musks, we might finally be able to solve this problem once and for all.

How?

The answer to this requires a little knowledge of economics.

The fundamental problem underlying all transactions is scarcity. In other words, an infinite number of demands must be met by a finite number of resources.

This leads to resource rationing that puts some above others. This problem proves unavoidable, however, as we're unable to increase the number of resources at our disposal.

That is—at least we think we are.

Musk's ideas of interplanetary space travel challenge this notion. In fact, if there were more Elon Musks in the world, we might have already eliminated the poverty problem.

When speaking of Elon Musk, it's easy to associate his ideas with science fiction. This one, however, borders on near fantasy—at least in the minds of many individuals.

However, with the right innovations, Musk's dream just may come to fruition. And it certainly wouldn't help to have a million more of him to help out.

So how, exactly, would having this many Elon Musks help eradicate poverty from the world?

In one fundamental way: we would be able to finally reach an infinite number of resources to meet our demands. This means that we would have enough to take care of everyone in the world so that no one had to live in poverty.

Now, this doesn't mean that there wouldn't be individuals who lived in excess or that there would be an even distribution of resources across the population.

However, poverty in the sense that individuals lack the basic necessities of life would no longer exist.

A muskmelon would do this by increasing the number of resources available by mining from other planets and using energy from the sun or a fusion reactor.

Musk's work through SolarCity has already made solar energy more affordable than before. By increasing its availability, a million Musks would be able to take this technology global. This would help raise the standard and the quality of life for millions living in poverty across the globe.

Just as importantly, Musk's ability to develop interplanetary space travel through SpaceX would increase the total number of resources available to us. And with a million genius entrepreneurs running around, these endeavors would already be well underway.

With that many Musks, there's no doubt that both the funding and the brainpower required to develop interplanetary space travel would already exist. This means that we would already be on the hunt for precious materials on other planets.

It could even mean increasing the total amount of farming and agricultural space to accommodate for the Earth's growing population.

In this way, it can be said that Musk's work is currently trending for the absolute abolition of poverty. And though steady progress has been made, one can only dream of the work that could be done if there were a million Elon Musks.

With an unlimited supply of resources taken from other planets—and with the world's energy needs solved through solar power—a utopian world could be created. And with a million Elon Musks, this world could be created sooner than anyone thought possible.

9. Save Humankind from Artificial Intelligence (AI)

Musk has joined the growing ranks of entrepreneurs and technological geniuses who have come out against the use of AI.

Calling AI a real threat to the safety of mankind; Musk created OpenAI. This secretive organization works to combat the growing threat of AI.

So, what, exactly, does OpenAI look to protect us from?

Get ready for one of the most bone-chilling of theories.

Musk and others with deep knowledge of AI now fear that we could soon have systems that can write their own code. In other words, they would have pure autonomy and could start far outpacing human intelligence.

So, what would that mean for us?

We would be left at the whim of hyperintelligent computer systems. We've already witnessed the astronomical growth of computer systems such as Watson that handily beat even the best of "Jeopardy!" champions. Other systems have bested world-class chess and go players, showing that AI has come a long way in competing with humans already.

The real fear, however, is that these machines will eventually develop the ability to replicate code at their own pace—something that Musk believes we're frighteningly close to seeing. This would mean that machines could develop their own intelligence and codes to do what they wanted to do.

And because they are processing information so quickly, we wouldn't be able to keep up.

This would lead to humans being replaced as apex predators. For those who think it sounds like science fiction, Musk and his supporters have another answer. With the development of OpenAI and Neuralink, Musk has already started developing high-end technology to combat fears of unstoppable artificial intelligence.

It's a move that Musk believes would make humans competitive against even the best AI systems. And it's one that humankind may be close to witnessing. In 2018, Musk stated that this first wave of Neuralink technology was on the verge of completion and would be "better" than anyone thought possible.

So that leaves us wondering: where would we be in this regard if we had a million Elon Musks? No matter how great AI has become, we're sure that it could reach the brainpower of so many incarnations of one of the world's leading geniuses.

In fact, with so many Elon Musks around, we're confident that Neuralink's mission would already be a success. This could feasibly make the world like a Marvel movie—we'd all be equipped with super intelligence.

The important part of this, however, would be that we'd be prepared for if—or when—AI rises to uncontrollable levels. And with a million Musks working to make sure that we stayed the apex predator, we're confident that we wouldn't lose our spot on the food chain any time soon.

The rest of the innovations these Musks could bring about can only be imagined. With both OpenAI and Neuralink operating in the shadows, it's hard to imagine what type of technology they may be secretly perfecting. We're sure that whatever it is, however, would already be completed with a million Musks working on it. In fact, we'd probably already have an even more updated version.

In short, with a million Elon Musks, the world would be a safer place. Instead of us being protected from outsiders, however, we'd be uniquely prepared to protect ourselves from our own creations.

The Bottom Line

The face of the world as we know it today would be unrecognizable with a million Elon Musks. With so many of this great innovator, it's almost a guarantee that Earth wouldn't even be our only home anymore.

With industry-leading technology being developed already at SpaceX, it's feasible that with more Musks working, we'd be an interplanetary species. Not only would we likely be enjoying commercialized travel to Mars—something that Musk predicts we'll enjoy within the next twenty or so years—we'd likely already have colonized the entire solar system.

But not all of the changes that would result from having a million Musks would be so far away. Some would have direct impacts on the quality of life here on Earth.

Mining from interplanetary travel, for instance, would work to eliminate world poverty. The commercialization of renewable energy would raise the standard of living for millions across the globe. More importantly, it would put an end to the ever-worsening climate crisis that affects our planet and the species that inhabit it.

What's more, Musk's dreams of revolutionizing travel here on Earth would already be in effect. This would lead to a large decrease in traffic—as well as travel at and more than the speed of sound. Even going cross country or to other countries could be done in a matter of minutes with Musk's Hyperloop and SpaceX's commercial rocket travel on Earth.

Even with all those impressive accomplishments in mind, having a million Elon Musks would also lead to an impressive upgrade to e-commerce. This original online payment pioneer would be able to revolutionize human monetary transactions several times over if he had a million clones of himself.

In short, a million Elon Musks would fundamentally change the human experience. By changing the ways, we understood space, travel, and even money, a million Elon Musks would alter our understanding of the world—just as one Elon Musk already has.

The world-famous and much-loved genius engineer works under a simple mantra: "When something is important enough, you do it even if the odds are not in your favor."

This is the attitude that has led Musk to make some of the most important inventions and innovations of our lifetime. No doubt, if more of us shared the same spirit, we could improve the world ten times over. This is a testament to the entrepreneur's character, work ethic, and vision, and it also speaks to a simple truth: the world needs more than one Elon Musk.

Important Books Everyone Should Read - Per Elon Musk (contd... 1/2)

Here is a list of must-read books that Elon Musk insists on. Though the books influencing Musk's life come from different genres, they broadly form three major segments: science fiction, AI & technology, and biographies.

Musk has been reading science fiction since childhood, which seems to be the reason for the curiosity about advanced science in his young mind. Among his favorite sci-fi novels, "The Hitchhiker's Guide to the Galaxy" by Douglas Adams is the one he read in South Africa in his teenage years. Combining science with comedy, this book creates a story of the Earth being devastated to create a way for the Galactic freeway. Arthur, the main hero, learns a lot from Ford Prefect (who turns out to be an alien later) about every planet in the Galaxy, and the reader gets a chance to explore his space travels. In homage to this book, Musk made the words "Don't Panic" appear on the dashboard of the Roadster during its launch into space. This shows how strongly a powerful reading experience can influence a person's life. Another of his favorites from sci-fi is the "Foundation" trilogy by Isaac Asimov, in which humans are settled across the Milky Way. This book is about a Galactic empire consisting of many planets built by humans. Another book in a similar context is "The Moon Is a Harsh Mistress" by Robert Heinlein. This book is about a dystopian future in which some humans are moved to the moon to create a libertarian community to rule the Earth. Musk's dream of settling on the other planet must have originated while reading these books. Next on the fiction list is "The Lord of the Rings" by J.R.R. Tolkien. Musk seems to have become fascinated by imagination and fiction after reading this series. Another thing he likes about this book is the aim of the heroes to save the world for a larger good. The last one on the sci-fi list is a series of ten books—The "Culture" series by Iain M. Banks, who narrates a real picture of our probable future regulated by machines. Fiction in this book appears to have inspired Elon Musk to bring it to reality.

In the technology segment, Elon Musk suggests two major books. One is "Superintelligence: Paths, Dangers, Strategies" by Nick Bostrom, which is for those who wish to know more about the latest technology, including AI, its impact on our future, and its creation. The second book is "Our Final Invention" by James Barrat, in which the author questions whether humans can live with artificially intelligent human replicas. Barrat even urges being careful while dealing with the coming generation of AI. Musk confesses with no hard feelings that AI may not be called evil even if it destroys humanity. It has an aim, and if humanity gets destroyed on its way, AI might not even think about it. We cannot deny the fact that AI is already here. The only thing we can choose is the direction in which it should go. This might have triggered Musk's vision of driverless cars and the electric car revolution. Musk also insists on reading "Life 3.0: Being Human in the Age of Artificial Intelligence" by Max Tegmark. While the previous two books on AI elaborate on the negative side, this book focuses on the positive side of artificial intelligence. It spreads the hope of furthering humanity through AI.

In the biography genre, Musk likes to read about people who lived extraordinary lives and achieved success based on what he calls their exceptional ability. The book "Benjamin Franklin: An American Life" by Walter Isaacson is one of these. Benjamin Franklin was an entrepreneur, according to Musk, who had nothing to start with, yet rose from shopkeeping to dining with the Royals. Franklin is one of the founding figures of the US and the inventor of many things, including lightning rods. He has been an inspirational personality in Musk's life while rising up from his struggling days. Another of his favorite biographies is "Einstein: His Life and Universe" by Walter Isaacson. Through Einstein's personal letters, this book captures his journey from a young, frustrated patent officer to a Nobel Prize winner. The author shines the light on the rebellious nature of that person in his young days still having a passion for what he believed in. Musk likes the way it impacts readers' minds to transform the way we see life. Elon Musk was fascinated by one more personality, Howard Hughes, and the awesomeness with which he lived his life. The book "Howard Hughes: His Life and Madness" by Donald L. Barlett and James B. Steele says that this man did not belong to this world. He was on a different tangent in terms of fame, finance, and success. For today's generation, Elon Musk is the modern-day Hughes.

Important Books Everyone Should Read - Per Elon Musk (...contd. 2/2)

Apart from these major genres, Musk loves reading books that focus on practical knowledge and its application. One of these books is "Structures: Or Why Things Don't Fall Down" by J.E. Gordon. Coming from a coding background, Musk was unsure of direct entry into making rockets. So, he started learning rocket science. From building up skyscrapers, suspended bridges, and other jaw-dropping stuff, this book answered all his questions about structural principles. This was an important read for Musk before sending heavy rockets into space. "Structures" was the book he used for learning how to build and stabilize the rocket. Now, for learning to ignite it and get it up from the ground, he referred to the book "Ignition: An Informal History of Liquid Rocket Propellants" by John D. Clark. As per Musk, ignition was a crucial part of the development of his rockets because it was related to fueling.

Musk's life is filled with startups and new ventures, one after the other. For those aiming to be like him, he recommends a book called "Zero to One: Notes on Startups, or How to Build the Future" by Peter Thiel, with whom Musk launched the company PayPal. In short, simple, and easy-to-read words, it highlights the point that new ideas, through startups, can change the world.

All his life, Elon Musk has been aiming at a sustainable future. Therefore, he supported the book "Merchants of Doubt" by Naomi Oreskes and Erik M. Conway in a tweet in 2013. This book attempts to uncover a bitter truth. Both the authors are scientists, and they write openly about the damage some companies are causing to the Earth and humans by using PR. Scientists are paid well and connected to politicians to mislead the public and hide important information from them. Musk, who aims for a better future, appreciates this courageous and truthful writing.

Looking at Musk's list of favorite books, it is clear that reading establishes a strong foundation for what a person becomes in life.

SECTION 2
ABOUT ELON MUSK AND
HIS COMPANIES

CHAPTER ONE

ELON MUSK: 21ST CENTURY REVOLUTIONARY

Overview

Fully-functioning electric cars. Trains that move at the speed of sound. Colonization of Mars.

Sound crazy? Not to Elon Musk.

Equal parts eccentric and brilliant, Elon Musk, is largely considered one of the visionaries of our time. Often called a "real-life Tony Stark," Musk is one of the world's most recognized figures and leads the push for futuristic technology.

Elon Musk has become a household name and a space-age symbol. Founder and CEO of futuristic companies such as Tesla (the world's leader in producing electric cars) and SpaceX (which seeks to redefine space technology and exploration), the celebrated engineer-entrepreneur, who has stated he would like to "die on Mars, just not on impact," has become a cultural icon and a leader in the digital and technological revolution.

Let's explore the life of one of the world's richest and most unpredictable men.

Early Life: "Raised by Books"

Elon Musk was born in Pretoria, South Africa, on June 28, 1971. The oldest of three siblings, Musk lived with his father Errol, an electromechanical engineer, and his Canadian-born mother Maye, a dietician, and model.

Musk's parents divorced when he was just ten years old; as a result, he would spend much of his childhood with his father. Reportedly, Musk decided to stay with his father out of pity. By all accounts, however,

Errol Musk was a stern man with a strong hand. This, combined with Elon Musk's introversion and his father's tendency to re-locate, made life tough at times for the future entrepreneur.

To further complicate matters, little Elon Musk rarely saw his parents. Instead, he spent the majority of his time at school or at home with an inattentive housekeeper. According to Musk, his family's housekeeper was hired more to make sure he didn't "break things" than to watch over him.

As such, the future Tesla CEO was free to explore his own interests. By Musk's own admission, he found an escape in books. In a 2017 *Rolling Stone* interview, Musk stated, "I was raised by books. Books, and then my parents."

While Musk's love of books and knowledge did not help him much at school—where he was a frequent target of bullying—it would become the catalyst for his future ingenuity. At the age of ten, Musk acquired a Commodore VIC-20. This inexpensive, dated computer allowed him his first foray into the world of programming.

Using his new computer, the adolescent Musk created a video game known as Blastar. Modeled after Space-Invaders, the game was good enough to earn young Elon $500 in a sale to PC and Office Technology magazine.

As the little entrepreneur coped with the absence of his parents by devouring books and developing computer programs at home, he faced unique challenges at school. Musk would graduate from Waterkloof House Preparatory School and later enroll in Pretoria Boys High School.

Musk doesn't remember the years fondly. The genius engineer stated, "I had a terrible upbringing. I had a lot of adversity growing up."

According to reports, Musk was a prime target of bullying at his school. Despite his intellectual prowess, teenage Musk never quite found his niche. Instead, he recalls the years in dark tones.

"For a number of years, there was no respite. You get chased around by gangs at school who tried to beat the (expletive) out of me, and then I'd come home, and it would just be awful there as well."

For years, Musk dreamed of escaping the rough Afrikaner lifestyle of South Africa by using his mother's connections to relocate to Canada. This dream became a reality at the age of seventeen when Musk officially left South Africa to start a new life in Canada.

His motive was simple: to escape the compulsory military service that would force him to participate in the dark Apartheid movement.

Musk would use his Canadian exit to start a new life and open doors that would bring him unprecedented success.

Education: PhD Dropout Turned Genius Entrepreneur

After graduating from Pretoria Boys High School in South Africa, Elon Musk enrolled at Queen's University in Canada at the age of seventeen. The year was 1989, and Musk was finally living his Canadian dream.

On his choice of university, Musk would later comment, "I was going to do physics and engineering at Waterloo… but there didn't seem to be any girls there! So, I visited Queen's, and there *were* girls there. I didn't want to spend my undergraduate time with a bunch of dudes."

Musk now brushes this off with a laugh, but there's no doubt that his stay in Kingston would have long-lasting impacts on his life. Recalling the place where he would eventually meet his first wife and mother of his five children, Musk stated, "I had a great time at Queen's… I'd call them formative years."

But the bright-eyed Musk did not stay in Kingston for long. Though he remembers his time at Queen's University fondly, Musk does not regret his decision to leave the school for the University of Pennsylvania.

Musk credits much of his success to the tools and information he gained at the university, where he earned a Bachelor of Science in Physics and a Bachelor of Arts in Economics from the world-renowned Wharton School.

Despite earning a double degree, Musk knew how to have fun. Keeping true to the values that led him to Queen's, the soon-to-be multimillionaire bought a ten-bedroom frat house with another Penn student and turned it into a nightclub.

Initially, the young Musk wished to pursue his education in energy physics. Indeed, Musk views physics as having a fundamental impact on his thinking and success. In a statement, the genius entrepreneur remarked that physics provides "a good framework for thinking... Boil things down to their fundamental truths and reason up from there."

With Musk's love of physics, it came as a surprise to no one that he applied for and was eventually accepted into a PhD program in the field at Stanford University.

What was shocking, however, was Musk's decision to pull out of the program only two days after enrolling. Embracing risk, Musk abandoned the certainty of higher education to pursue a career in Internet technology.

At just twenty-four years of age, young Elon Musk stared face-first into a sea of opportunity with a vision of changing the world.

Zip2: Musk's First Success

With a mind at capitalizing on the growing Internet market, Elon Musk teamed up with his brother Kimbal Musk and entrepreneur Greg Kouri to start Zip2 in 1995. How the brothers obtained startup costs for their first venture is still up for debate. What's clear is that significant cash was obtained from angel investors, while $6,000 of Kouri's own money was funneled into the project.

Despite some reports that Elon's father Errol Musk donated $28,000 in startup funds, Elon Musk denies the claim. In fact, in his 2017 *Rolling Stone* interview, Musk paints quite a different picture of his father's philanthropy.

"One thing he claims is he gave us a whole bunch of money to start…our first company. This is not true. He was irrelevant. He paid nothing for college…[and] the funding we raised for our first company came from a small group of random angel investors…"

While the exact details of Zip2's creation are unknown, it's undeniable that the company marked Musk's first major success as an entrepreneur.

But what was Zip2?

Unlike Musk's later ventures, the business had little to do with futuristic cars or space travel. Instead, it served as an early bridge for print newspapers and the online medium. Specifically, Musk envisioned a company that could help local businesses and newspapers find an online identity.

Initially, the company, which was started as Global Link Information Network, aided local businesses in establishing an Internet presence. Over time, however, the company began helping newspaper publishers design online city guides that could be used to expand their outreach.

The company would change its name to Zip2 in 1996 after significant investments from Mohr Davidow Ventures. As part of the change, Musk was given the title of Chief Technology Officer.

Zip2 eventually secured contracts with industry heavyweights such as *The New York Times* and the *Chicago Tribune*. In doing so, the company became a major player in the field and served as Musk's first successful business venture.

Despite this, the board steadfastly blocked Musk's attempts at becoming CEO and sold the company just four years after its inception. Zip2 was eventually bought out by Compaq for the whopping sum of $307 million. At the time of the sale, the company worked with nearly 160 newspapers.

As a founder, Musk received a 7% commission off the sale or a value that was equal to twenty-two million dollars. Despite the loss of his first company, Musk was quick to invest his money into new avenues.

X.com: Revolutionizing Online Banking

Spurred by his success with Zip2, Elon Musk founded X.com in November 1999. Musk's X.com was one of the world's first online banking services and was designed to provide consumers with the convenience of banking on the go.

As part of Musk's strategy, all X.com deposits were insured by the FDIC, as they would be with any traditional brick-and-mortar bank. Musk, who had invested twelve million dollars of his own wealth into the company, was undaunted as many of his initial team left the business to form their own brands.

Instead, Musk focused on finding ways to grow his online banking service. As part of this, the multimillionaire employed a variety of online marketing schemes that are still highly-effective today. Anyone who signed up with X.com received a $20 cash card; those who referred friends to the service received a $10 cash card.

These marketing schemes helped X.com grow and compete in the field of online banking. In order to compete with its rivals, Musk shifted focus to online transaction systems that would allow customers to transfer money through email.

Shortly after, Musk approved a merger with the company's biggest rival, Confinity. Confinity and X.com had been in a months-long battle that saw tough competition between their major services and products. Eventually, however, Confinity was forced to bow to X.com as the company began running low on cash. Because X.com was the more financially stable of the two companies, Musk was appointed CEO of the newly-merged business, which kept the name X.com.

As CEO of X.com, Musk presided over Confinity's recently-launched PayPal, a service that was designed to help individuals send money through email. Initially, X.com had worked to compete against Confinity and their PayPal service with their own online person-to-person money transaction service. When the two companies merged, however, the focus shifted to the development of Confinity's original PayPal system. Under Musk's leadership, PayPal was formed into the service we recognize today.

Despite this, X.com's infrastructure could not keep up with a growing client base. Crashes and bugs plagued the online service, and those on the opposite side of the merger began to doubt Musk's readiness to be a CEO.

In a shocking move, Musk would be ousted from his role while on vacation to Africa. By all reports, Musk had been replaced in the role by Peter Thiel, a co-founder of Confinity, before his plane had even landed. Though Musk immediately flew back to the United States and attempted to sell the board on his worth, his attempts were denied.

X.com would later be renamed PayPal. Despite being ousted from his role, Musk continued to invest in PayPal, a service he believed could revolutionize the financial market. PayPal was eventually bought out by eBay in 2002 for a whopping 1.5 billion dollars. Musk, who at one time was the company's primary stockholder, received $167 million from his eleven percent share in the company.

In 2017, Musk purchased the domain X.com from PayPal in a sale that was reportedly worth millions of dollars. In a tweet, the genius said, "Thanks PayPal for allowing me to buy back X.com! No plans right now, but it has great sentimental value to me."

Whether or not Musk plans to start a new venture under the classic name is yet to be seen.

Tesla: The Future of Automobiles

Though a pioneer for many ambitious projects, Musk is perhaps best known for co-founding Tesla.

Musk currently serves as the co-founder and CEO of the company, where he oversees the production and the design of every product.

Tesla was founded in July 2003, and Musk, who had recently founded Internet giant PayPal, quickly began sizeable financial contributions to the organization.

Martin Eberhard and Marc Tarpenning founded Tesla in 2003. The company draws its name from Serbian-American scientist Nikola Tesla and initially looked to combat a recall of electric cars by GM.

Though in reality, Musk did not found the company, his sizeable financial contributions during series A funding in February 2004 led him to become the chairman of the board of directors. Along with two others, Musk also earned retroactive founder status.

Musk quickly became the face of the Tesla brand. His quick wit and ingenuity led him to oversee the production of Tesla's first commercialized electric vehicle, the Roadster.

The genius engineer-entrepreneur remained heavily involved in both the funding of Tesla and its production during initial funding.

In total, Musk contributed over $30 million to Tesla during the funding period, becoming the controlling investor of the company early in its history.

Despite his financial involvement and his work on the Roadster, Musk remained distant from the day-to-day operations of the business.

It wasn't until 2008 that Musk would cement his legacy at Tesla. It was then that he succeeded co-founder Eberhard as CEO and product architect for the company. Eberhard's departure followed plummeting profits and rising problems after the 2008 financial crisis.

Under Musk's leadership, Tesla has become a prospering company, with an estimated value of over $600 billion.

Soon after Musk took charge, Tesla released their first electric vehicle—the Tesla Roadster. It proved a success for Musk, as he remained heavily involved in product engineering.

Though the Roadster sold only around 2,500 vehicles, Tesla reached thirty-one markets.

Since then, Tesla has added additional electric vehicles to its collection. These include the Model S in June 2012, the Model X in September 2015, the Model 3 in July 2017, and the Model Y in March 2019. The Tesla Semi, an all-electric battery-powered Class 8 semi-truck in development, was unveiled in November 2017. The Cybertruck, an all-electric, battery-powered, pick-up truck, and the Cyberquad, an all-terrain vehicle (ATV), were unveiled in November 2019. Within just 5-days, the Cybertruck received 250,000 pre-orders. The Cybertruck was developed to provide a sustainable-energy substitute for the roughly 6,500 fossil-fuel-powered trucks sold per day in the United States.

Under Musk's direction, Tesla's new series of vehicles cater to both average and luxury consumers, expanding the company's reach into new kinds of markets.

The company also remains committed to expanding access to electric cars. In May 2013, for instance, Tesla noted that they were upping production of their supercharger stations. The move would make it easier for electric car owners to charge their vehicles throughout the nation.

The following year, Musk made a good-faith announcement that would allow others to use their technology patents to aid in electric car development. The move sought to ease the burden of building electric cars for traditional manufacturers.

Musk's time at Tesla hasn't been without controversy, however. The entrepreneur made headlines in September 2018 for a possible drug-induced tweet that caught the attention of the U.S. Securities and Exchange Commission (SEC).

In a controversial move, Musk announced via Twitter that he had secured funds to take Tesla private at $420 a share. Allegations arose at the time that Musk had no intentions of making the company private. Instead, they alleged, the tweet came as a way to manipulate the stock market in the company's favor.

Musk denied the claims, but the SEC eventually found the CEO and product architect of Tesla, Inc culpable. As part of a settlement reached with the SEC, Musk and Tesla were forced to pay a $20 million fine, and Musk stepped down from his position as chairman of the company. He was succeeded by Robyn Denholm but still retains his status as the company's CEO.

Musk's tweets drew even more scrutiny when it was alleged by rapper Azalea Banks that they were fueled by LSD.

The rapper, who noted that she had been at Musk's house at the time, recalled hearing conversations that would have landed the entrepreneur in hot water.

Banks distinctly recalled Musk taking LSD at the time of the tweets and hearing him on the phone "scrounging for investors."

The SEC considered Banks' statements in their settlement with Musk.

Additionally, as part of their settlement, Tesla directors were called to keep an eye on their CEO's tweets.

Tweets made in February 2019, however, suggested that the company was falling short of its duties.

The Tesla CEO tweeted that the company expected to produce 500,000 cars in 2019—comparing it to the zero produced in 2011.

The tweet quickly caught the eye of investors, however, as production was over 100,000 more than previously indicated by the company. Four hours later, Musk issued a correction of his original tweet, putting the numbers back in line with initial company projections.

Though it bore no repercussions, the move was widely criticized by commentators. They felt as if it were another attempt to manipulate the market by forecasting better results than what was initially expected. At the time of the tweets, however, the markets had already closed.

Musk, who has gained a reputation as an eccentric genius entrepreneur, has defended his tweeting style. As Tesla continues to grow, the entrepreneur's tweeting habits will likely continue to come under continued scrutiny.

Despite this, Musk's success at Tesla cannot be denied. Musk, who owns roughly 22% of Tesla stock, has led the company to become one of the leading producers of electrical products. Additionally, Musk's drive has led to Tesla securing big-name partnerships, including Mercedes-Benz and Toyota.

SpaceX: Commercializing Interplanetary Travel

Perhaps no project better highlights Musk's ambition than SpaceX.

With the founding of SpaceX in 2002, Musk made one thing clear:

He wanted to commercialize space travel.

Since its inception, SpaceX has become a leading aerospace manufacturer and has made long strides towards the commercialization of space travel.

Musk, who oversees production, led the company to launch its first rocket to reach orbit in 2008. In 2010, they hit another milestone when they became the first privately-funded company to successfully launch, orbit, and recover a spaceship.

Following their success in 2008, Musk established a partnership with NASA. Under their agreement, SpaceX received permission to deliver both cargo and crew to the International Space Station (ISS). Since then, SpaceX has conducted twenty resupply missions and successfully launched their first crewed mission in May 2020.

The company's success rests largely on Musk's ambition.

"If humanity is to become multi-planetary," the genius is reported to have said by *The Texas Tribune*, "the fundamental breakthrough that needs to occur in rocketry is a rapidly and completely reusable rocket."

It's perhaps this belief that led SpaceX to become the first company—private or otherwise—to successfully launch and recover a reusable rocket in 2017.

The company's multi-planetary goals received another boon in September of 2016 when Musk announced its upcoming Interplanetary Transport System.

The goal of this privately-funded program is simple yet ambitious: develop equipment and technology to allow for crewed interplanetary flight.

In 2017, Musk announced that the system had been renamed to "Starship and Super Heavy."

In the same announcement, Musk revealed that the program's first project was the development of a reusable rocket. This rocket, planned to be the largest ever developed, is scheduled for release in the late 2020s.

At that time, Musk intends to conduct the company's first mission to Mars. It's an interplanetary mission that Musk hopes will one day be commercialized.

"I'm confident moving to Mars (return ticket is free) will one day cost less than $500k & maybe even below $100k," he tweeted in early February of 2019.

It's a move that Musk says would allow "most people in advanced economies [to] sell their home on Earth & move to Mars if they want."

For many, Musk's ideas seem to be no more of a reality than the science fiction novels he coveted as a child.

But for Musk, SpaceX has become the avenue by which he can accomplish his childhood dreams. The same student captivated by *The Hitchhiker's Guide to the Galaxy* now seeks to be the man to commercialize interplanetary space travel.

And the company has already made massive leaps in doing it.

Musk's planned Starship will be 180 feet tall. Super Heavy, the rocket launcher that will carry it into orbit, will be an impressive 220 feet tall— meaning that it will be the largest rocket ever developed upon its debut.

The ship, which is designed to carry up to 100 tons of cargo and 100 passengers at a time, will rely on game-changing innovations.

All from the mind of one of the 21st-century's greatest and most-innovative entrepreneurs.

Musk recently announced reduced costs for the project, citing that a switch to stainless steel body would save the company costs.

To combat the harsh atmospheres of Earth and Mars, Musk led a development team to create a "radical" new way to protect the ship.

"What I want to do is have the first-ever regenerative heat shield," he said in an interview with *Popular Mechanics*. "A double-walled stainless shell—like a stainless-steel sandwich, essentially, with two layers."

It's this design that allows for Musk to include his latest innovation.

"You just need two layers that are joined with stringers," he continued. "You flow either fuel or water in between the sandwich layer ... and you essentially bleed water, or you could bleed fuel, through the micro-perforations on the outside."

It is something Musk believed will allow for the rocket to maintain a cool enough temperature to avoid melting while traveling through planetary atmospheres. The plan was abandoned a few months later in favor of thin ceramic tiles as a heat shield for the windward side of the starship.

Those who question the success of Musk's idea will get their first glimpse of it in action in 2021.

Musk announced that SpaceX looks to test a small Hopper prototype that will provide more insight into the project's direction.

Unfortunately, this small-scale test won't actually go into space, but Musk and his developers will get a chance to test it in the Earth's atmosphere.

If successful, Musk's wild dreams of interplanetary travel will be one step closer to reaching fruition. With a successful launch, Musk and SpaceX may once again prove revolutionary.

Hyperloop: Transportation of the Future

In July 2012, Musk unveiled the nature of his current project, the Hyperloop. Donning it the "fifth mode of transportation," Musk stated this new form of passenger railway could significantly change modern transportation.

Designed by Musk and teams from his Tesla and SpaceX companies, the Hyperloop consists of a passenger train running through vacuum tubing. In theory, the train, which would be immune to collisions, weather, and the outside environment, would levitate off the tracks in underground or above ground tubing. Because the train would move without friction, Musk predicts that it will be able to carry passengers to their destinations at the speed of sound.

Though the idea was criticized by some as science fiction, Musk announced in 2015 that SpaceX would build a mile-long test track. The Founder, CEO, and Lead Designer of SpaceX also opened a competition to companies and student teams to see who could build the best Hyperloop prototype. The competition would be the first of its kind, with a second phase taking place in 2017.

Using electrodynamic suspension and eddy current braking, the MIT Hyperloop Team became the competition's first winner, developing the first successful Hyperloop prototype. The pod developed by the MIT team would also be the first to successfully perform a low-pressure Hyperloop run.

According to Musk, the Hyperloop would be able to transport passengers from San Francisco to Los Angeles in thirty minutes. In other words, the Hyperloop would move at about double the speed of passenger aircraft.

Musk sees this as just the first step, however, noting that later Hyperloop models may be able to move at "hypersonic speed." This has led to concerns over the safety and feasibility of the system.

Furthermore, critics doubt the current six-billion-dollar price tag for the Hyperloop, suggesting that the true costs of developing and implementing the infrastructure necessary to run such a system will be much higher.

As of December 10, 2018, two miles of a test track for Musk's hyperloop have been laid and are ready for further testing.

Personal Life: Musk's Best Kept Secret

Perhaps one of Musk's greatest achievements has been his ability to keep his personal life private.

Despite being one of the most influential entrepreneurs of the 21st century, Musk has avoided the personal spotlight.

From what is known about his personal life, however, one may conclude that it's not been quite as successful as his professional career.

For instance, Musk has been divorced three times and has a rocky relationship with his father.

A busy entrepreneur, Musk wed his first wife, Justine Wilson, at the age of 29 in 2000. Their relationship, however, suffered serious setbacks—mainly after the death of their first child.

The couple first met at Queen's University in Ontario when Musk offered to buy her ice cream. Despite initial rejection, the pair would soon enter an eight-year marriage.

The death of their first son of sudden infant death syndrome (SIDS) proved an insurmountable obstacle in their relationship. Though the couple would go on to have five children together—one set of twins and a set of triplets—they never got over the loss of their son.

The two slowly drifted apart until Musk filed for divorce in 2008. Wilson now claims that she no longer has direct contact with Musk and instead conducts her discussions through an assistant.

Musk's first divorce undoubtedly proved a tough loss for the 37-year-old entrepreneur. In a 2017 interview with *Rolling Stone*, Musk admitted that he needs love to feel happy.

"If I'm not in love, if I'm not with a long-term companion, I cannot be happy," he said in his interview. "I will never be happy without having someone."

It's a problem that seems to be compounded by Musk's financial success.

"Being in a big empty house, and the footsteps echoing through the hallway, no one there and no one on the pillow next to you … How do you make yourself happy in a situation like that?"

That's perhaps why Musk wasted no time in entering his second marriage in 2010. Musk's new bride, Talulah Riley, proved less compatible for the entrepreneur than Wilson.

Musk and Riley would eventually split up after only two years in 2012. However, their rocky relationship got new life when the couple married again in 2013.

This time, their relationship would survive another three years. But turbulence at home would lead to the couple getting a final divorce in 2016.

It was during this time that Musk met his next partner—Amber Heard. Heard, the former wife of renowned actor Johnny Depp, was also recently divorced.

The pair would quickly enter into an on-again, off-again relationship that ultimately ended in February 2018. Unlike with his former partners, Musk never tied the knot with Heard, and the two reportedly kept contact after the breakup.

Musk's relationship with Heard reveals just how rocky his personal life may really be. Only about a year into the relationship, Musk and Heard split in 2017. At the time, the pair cited busy schedules as the reason behind their breakup.

They found time for each other in January of 2018, however, as the couple once again began to date.

But it was only a month later that Musk reportedly ended the relationship.

The move proves surprising when looking at Musk's comments to the *Rolling Stone* in regard to the couple's initial breakup.

"Well, she broke up with me more than I broke up with her, I think," he said three months after their August 2017 split. "I was really in love, and it hurt bad."

Since the pair's most recent parting, Musk entered another relationship in May 2018 with Claire Elise Boucher (professionally known as Grimes). She is a Canadian singer and producer. Surprisingly, the couple met on Twitter, and shortly after, they debuted as a couple at the Met Gala.

The couple has faced many ups and downs in the past two years as they even suffered a temporary breakup. However, in February, Grimes revealed she is expecting a baby boy that she gave birth to just a few months later.

Musk announced the name of his baby boy on Twitter as X Æ A-12, and soon enough, he became the subject of many memes across the Internet. The couple is happy and thriving as of now.

The 47-year-old entrepreneur's trouble with relationships extends to more than his romantic involvements.

In an uncharacteristic tell-all interview, Musk admitted to having an estranged relationship with his father, Errol Musk.

Musk has characterized his father as a "terrible human being" and expounded upon this notion in his bombshell interview.

"You have no idea about how bad," he said, speaking of his father. "Almost every crime you can possibly think of, he has done. Almost every evil thing you can possibly think of, he has done."

Musk, who reportedly has not spoken to his father in over a year, may have good reason to do so. The elder Musk recently fathered a son with his own stepdaughter—a woman he had known and had helped raise since she was four.

The engineering genius drew national ire in September 2018 when he smoked weed live during an interview on the *Joe Rogan Podcast*.

While he drew support from many wishing for the legalization of cannabis, Musk faced an unintended backlash from others. Critics noted that Musk routinely drug tested his Tesla employees and that he held himself to a different standard than the common worker.

Reports of other drug use by Musk draw further scrutiny into the genius entrepreneur's personal habits. At times—such as during his Tesla tweets —this drug use may have reportedly landed him in legal trouble.

For those looking to keep up with this active engineer-entrepreneur, consider following this:

Musk stays active on his Twitter account (@elonmusk) and can be followed at https://twitter.com/elonmusk

What's Next: Anyone's Guess

What's next for the genius entrepreneur? It's hard to say. With recent startups such as The Boring Company and Neuralink, the eccentric visionary does not appear to be slowing down any time soon.

In addition to his involvement in several startups, Musk also serves in an executive role in Solar City, a company that serves to redefine energy use across America and the globe.

With his hand on several projects, it's impossible to say what direction Elon Musk will move in next. Whatever the case, we can be sure that with each action, the cultural icon will take us one step closer to the future. Whether colonizing Mars or developing transportation systems that move beyond the speed of sound, Elon Musk is paving the way for a brighter, more technological future. The rest of us are just in for the ride.

Elon Musk Has 6 Sons and 0 Daughters!

Elon Musk actually had seven sons, the first of whom, named Nevada Alexander Musk, died as an infant. Later, his ex-wife, Justine Musk, gave birth to five sons—first to twins and then to triplets. Recently, Elon Musk and Grimes had a baby boy in 2020, which made Musk the father of six sons. You must be wondering why Elon Musk's kids are only boys, with no girls. The argument behind it is as logical as Musk himself. Let's look at a very scientific yet interesting fact about his life.

Because mothers give birth to a baby, it was considered for many years that the gender of the baby was dependent on the mother's biology. Over a period of time, scientific discovery confirmed that the person responsible for the baby's gender is actually the father. Additionally, it has been proved that a male carries the XY chromosome, whereas a female carries XX chromosomes. Hence, male sperm can carry either an X or Y chromosome, and a female egg (ovum) always carries an X chromosome. If a sperm contributes an X chromosome, it results in a girl, whereas if it contributes a Y chromosome, a baby boy is born. To add more to this research, Newcastle University conducted a family study in North America and Europe, which involved analysis of as many as 927 family trees and statistics about 556,387 individuals.

After an in-depth investigation, this study concluded that the tendency to have sons or daughters is genetically acquired by a male from his parents. The lead researcher at Newcastle University, Corry Gellatly, reveals that men who have more brothers possess a greater possibility of having sons. Similarly, men who have more sisters possess a greater possibility of having daughters. However, this is unpredictable in the case of women.

Another point the study puts forward is that there is an undiscovered gene in our bodies that regulates the X or Y chromosomes in a man's sperm. That means it is this undiscovered gene that conclusively determines the gender of the baby.

A gene inherits one part from each parent. So, the gene consists of two parts; each part is termed an allele. Accordingly, men bear two different types of alleles, resulting in three probable combinations in a gene. As per a Science Daily report, the ratio of X and Y sperm is under the control of these combinations in a gene.

The first combination lets out more Y sperm, which leads to the birth of sons. The second combination lets out roughly equal numbers of X and Y sperm, creating the equal possibility of sons as well as daughters. The reason for seeing approximately equal numbers of men and women in a population is that the gene is passed from both parents and causes some men to get more sons and some men to get more daughters.

Now you know why Musk has six sons and no daughters! His genetic structure has a higher possibility of releasing more Y sperm, resulting in a baby boy.

CHAPTER TWO

COMPANIES ASSOCIATED WITH OR FOUNDED BY ELON MUSK

Introduction

Elon Musk is one of the most successful serial entrepreneurs of our lifetime.

In fact, we have nearly lost count of all the businesses he's started. It seems like everything the eccentric engineer-entrepreneur touches turns to gold. From small, Internet-based newspaper directories to multi-billion-dollar space companies that aim to put humans on Mars, Musk has proven himself time and again one of the most accomplished men of our age.

In this chapter, we'll cover every major business Elon Musk has ever been associated with. Journey with us as we go through the time and look at the details of each of the genius entrepreneur's successful enterprises.

Ready? Let's begin!

Zip2

Founded in 1995 as Global Link Information Network, Zip2 was Elon Musk's first business venture. The company was a huge risk on Musk's part—apparently worth more than a Stanford education.

While the origins of this company are not clear, it's no secret that Zip2 was a massive success. So, what was this landmark first business for one of the world's richest men?

It was perhaps simpler than you may think. When founded, Zip2 (or Global Link) helped brick-and-mortar businesses establish an online presence.

While this may not sound special today, it was a groundbreaking service when it was established in the mid-1990s.

The company would undergo massive changes a year after its inception, as significant investment from Mohr Davidow Ventures led to a renaming and restructuring of the corporation. Following these investments, the company would be renamed Zip2, and its fundamental business practices would change. While Global Link had focused on helping businesses find an online identity, Zip2 would sell software to consumers (mainly print publishers) who wished to make their own directories.

With its new slogan "We Power the Press," Zip2 boomed in the online print industry, securing deals with national heavyweights such as *The New York Times* and *The Chicago Tribune*. Soon, Zip2 was recognized as one of the forefront online guides for newspaper directories in the United States.

Institutionalized changes following the renaming would see Elon Musk appointed as Chief Technology Officer. This left the CEO position open to Rich Sorkin, who would run the company until its eventual buyout by Compaq. In 1998, the year before the buyout, Zip2 worked with nearly 160 newspapers, developing extensive city guides.

Additionally, the company worked in some capacity to connect online newspaper users to physical car dealerships in their area. This was achieved through a program known as Auto Guide. In some instances, Auto Guide would also connect users with private individuals who wished to sell their cars.

Much communication between users and advertisers was done through fax. These faxes were available in print and at specific, predetermined URLs.

Before eventually allowing a merger with Compaq in 1999, Elon Musk blocked an attempted merger between Zip2 and its rival CitySearch. Though Musk initially supported the move, he would later tell the board of directors that the two companies were incompatible. Fearing the worst, the board denied the merger but kept their eyes open for potential opportunities.

One came less than a year later, when, in February of 1999, Compaq purchased the company for a sum of $307 million. Upon the merger, Zip2 would disappear entirely, serving only to improve Compaq's AltaVista search engine.

As part of the merger, both Musk brothers netted millions of dollars, marking their first success. For Elon in particular, Zip2 would become the first of many entrepreneurial success stories.

PayPal/X.com

Immediately following the Zip2/Compaq merger, Elon Musk channeled his energy and funds into a different venture. His next project would be riskier and more large-scale than his first, and it would be backed by twelve million dollars of his own money.

With this multi-million-dollar investment, Musk became the company's largest shareholder. He would name his company X.com and would become its first CEO. X.com functioned as an FDIC-insured online bank that allowed customers to make deposits online.

According to reports, X.com was one of the first online banks in the world. Still, the service faced tough competition from businesses like Confinity, which sought to revolutionize the game with an individual money transfer system known as PayPal. The idea behind PayPal was simple: Palm Pilot users would be able to send money to each other through their devices.

As the service grew, it advanced from Palm Pilots to the Internet. Confinity's PayPal soon offered payment services through email links. In order to keep up, Musk's X.com began to offer its own email-based payment transfer system.

The competition didn't last long. In March of 2000, less than one year after the formation of X.com, the two companies merged. At the time, Confinity was not in good economic shape. As a result, Musk retained his status as CEO, and the name of X.com was chosen over Confinity. In his expanded role, Musk worked to oversee the growth of Confinity's original PayPal system.

By all accounts, Musk believed PayPal to be the payment option of the future. As such, the young millionaire worked to see it grow into an internationally-accepted payment transaction system. Unfortunately, Musk's tenure as CEO was marked by severe deficiencies and conflict. Despite growing the company by hundreds of employees and helping put Confinity's original PayPal service on the map, Musk wasn't without his share of issues as CEO of the company.

Specifically, members of X.com began to doubt Musk's ability to lead. This was especially true for those on the Confinity side of the merger. Beliefs that Musk was holding the company back and squandering opportunity ran rampant. Worse, X.com was losing significant amounts of money due to fraud and operational deficiencies that resulted from a growing user base. Speculation that the company couldn't survive under Musk's leadership cast the future of X.com into doubt.

In a move that shocked the corporate world, Musk was booted from his role as CEO one day while on a flight to Africa for vacation. The move saw Peter Thiel, a co-founder and former CEO of Confinity, replace Musk as CEO of X.com.

Under Thiel's leadership, X.com would change its name to PayPal in June of 2001. The service built itself around online payment transactions and would eventually be bought out by eBay for a massive sum of $1.5 billion. Luckily for Musk, this meant some serious cash.

Tesla

Perhaps Musk's best-known company, Tesla, is an electric car company specializing in the production of luxury and mainstream electric vehicles. As of today, Tesla is the world's leading electric automobile producer and works as well to create solar roof tiles, solar installations, and energy storage-related products.

Interestingly, however, Tesla was not founded by Elon Musk. Conceptualized by Martin Eberhard and Marc Tarpenning, the company was originally called Tesla Motors (a name shortened to just "Tesla" in 2017). Inspiration for the company stemmed from the recall of General Motor's electric cars; Eberhard and Tarpenning desired to capitalize on the automobile giant's miss to create their own line of efficient electric cars.

In 2004, multi-millionaire Elon Musk came aboard during Series A funding for the project. Musk, who had long wished to foray into the realm of technology, put up $30 million of his own money to fund the venture. In doing so, he was appointed chairman, while Eberhard and Tarpenning operated as CEO and CFO, respectively.

The company wished to create an electric sports car that could compete with gasoline-powered options. This vision became a reality in 2008 when Tesla Motors unveiled its Roadster design. The car used lithium-ion cells to power an electric motor that could carry the vehicle a distance of 245 miles per charge. In nearly every performance metric, this groundbreaking electric car matched its gasoline-powered rivals, and with a price tag of nearly $110,000, it was considered the best electric sports car to date.

Despite the success of the Roadster, both original founders left the company in 2008. It is believed that Elon Musk played a prominent role in the booting of Martin Eberhard from his position as CEO of Tesla Motors. It was no secret that the two held various disagreements over the design of their Roadster model.

Reports also surfaced that Musk was not happy with his lack of credit for Tesla's success. Major news outlets slighted Musk, who felt that Eberhard was getting too much (unearned) credit. According to reports, a contentious relationship grew between the two.

Following Eberhard's exit, outsider Michael Marks was appointed interim CEO. In this role, Marks worked simply to not "rock the boat." Marks would serve as CEO until such time that a suitable replacement could be found. His replacement, as it turned out, was Musk. From 2008 until 2012, Musk oversaw the extensive growth of the company through the success of the Roadster.

In 2012, however, Tesla Motors halted production of its signature vehicle to begin production on a new model. Titled Model S, this sedan option would feature three different battery options and allow consumers to drive up to 300 miles on a single charge. Unlike the Roadster, this vehicle's battery would be located under the floorboards, giving passengers more room and the car a more natural feel.

Tesla would ride this success and create another vehicle: Model X. Model X bills itself as the safest SUV ever, and with seven-person seating, it is one of the most popular and innovative Tesla options to date. With the company's growing success, Tesla became the leading electric cars distributor in the world in 2018. This distinction comes in addition to Tesla's growth in other markets.

Model 3 is Tesla's first mass-market luxury all-electric four-door sedan. Within a week of unveiling the Model 3 in 2016, Tesla revealed they had taken 325,000 reservations for the car. Following crash testing, it received five stars in every category from the National Highway Traffic Safety Administration. The Model 3 Standard Range version delivers an EPA-rated all-electric range of 220 miles (354 km), and the Long-Range version delivers 325 miles (523 km). The Model 3 has a minimalist dashboard with only a center-mounted LCD touchscreen. Tesla stated that the Model 3 carries full self-driving hardware to be optionally enabled at a future date.

It took Tesla at least six months longer than expected to manufacture 5,000 units of this very ambitious electric sedan per week. There were failures at the Fremont facility, the most noticeable one being the removal of a detailed conveyor belt system that was replaced with workers. This resulted in the manufacturing process being thirty percent less productive than what Tesla anticipated at the beginning.

The delivery of Model 3 was delayed considerably as a result of the aggressive timeline. Since the failures during the production ramp of Model 3, Tesla has never stopped trying to improve its efficiency, and this alone is why it's a company worth supporting. It still manages to prosper and realize world-class results.

It turns out that what was originally deemed as an entire bet of the company ended up within one year becoming the 15th best-selling passenger car in the U.S.—gas-powered or electric—next to long-time industry staples like the Ford F-150 and Toyota RAV4.

Little did the world know, Musk was well on his way to producing some of the most efficient vehicles—even next to the most fuel-efficient and more affordable gas-powered vehicles—and becoming one of the most valuable companies on the planet.

On March 14, 2019, Tesla unveiled its new compact SUV called Model Y to widespread anxiety. Model Y was announced as an affordable electric car that can travel 225 miles on a single charge.

Model Y was greatly based on the Model 3 sedan—so similarly that Tesla was basically accused of fraud. Its unveiling was downplayed, and those with financial involvement with the company were not happy that Model Y shared 75% of the same parts and features as the Model 3. The only major difference was that it offered more headroom in the rear seating.

Additionally, Model Y required a $2,500 deposit, whereas Model 3 only required a $1,000 deposit. Investors felt cheated, and this is why Tesla stock dipped nearly three percent after the unveiling.

With the long anticipation between the unveil and delivery of Model Y, consumers remained hesitant to put money down early for it. This same notion didn't result in many benefits during the Model 3 unveil, so why should consumers have felt inclined to do so this time around? Not to mention there were no stunning additions to Model Y that made it stand out other than it appearing to be a Model 3 hatchback. There was no new enthusiasm for Tesla's brand. This meant that Tesla actually *needed* to sell units for its stock to perform.

Despite what investors originally thought: The Model Y unveil being more of a money grab to fund their next endeavor, the crossover SUV exceeded expectations during ramp. This time, Tesla started with a more reasonable timeline for delivery that it knew it could comfortably beat.

There were unsatisfactory reviews during delivery of Model Y that continued from Model 3, such as the panel gaps and the screen remaining cluttered and still sitting off-center. Tesla also failed to heighten the driving experience from Model 3 that actually wasn't a concern with both Model S and Model X. Model 3 and Model Y both presented stiff rides and wind noise inside the cabin.

A major deficiency Model Y held was that with its "Traffic Light and Stop Sign Control" function, it would stop at red, yellow, and green lights if other vehicles were in view, making drivers feel unsafe in urban areas. Through this function, Tesla vehicles have also been known to arrive at stop signs at full speed and then stop suddenly. It appears that this function—a part of the "Autopilot" feature—lacks accuracy when scanning scenes to look for signs and signals. Musk has since promised that these blemishes will be refined as Tesla prepares to launch fully functional self-driving electric vehicles by the end of 2020. With these flaws still not entirely weaned out and with the constant updates, it takes away from relaxation and the safety that "Autopilot" is actually supposed to offer. Despite the numerous setbacks, Tesla delivered its one-millionth vehicle in March 2020.

On August 28, 2020, Tesla began offering its own in-house insurance service for its vehicles, containing comprehensive coverage and claims management. It's currently offered in California with plans of expansion to all U.S. consumers in the future. Tesla insurance holders can expect up to at least twenty percent lower rates than competitors.

Tesla Insurance offers lower rates because through this method, Tesla knows their own vehicles. They know the ins and outs of the advanced technology, safety, and serviceability of their cars like no other insurance provider would.

From the first delivery of Model 3 to now, the buzz around Tesla comes entirely from word of mouth. Tesla hasn't paid a cent for their advertising, ever. Tesla's priority investment opportunities don't lie in running the most creative multi-million-dollar marketing campaigns like their competitors. Rather, their funds are used to develop tomorrow's ingenuity—think "fund forward."

In November 2019, Tesla revealed its anticipated Cybertruck. What viewers didn't expect was that Musk also revealed an all-terrain vehicle (ATV) that fits onto the Cyber pickup truck's six-and-a-half-foot bed. This further exhibits the truck's "Tesla-esque" move of adding a charging outlet for the ATV above the truck's right rear tire. The ATV holds 32 kW (43 horsepower), it can hit up to 70 miles per hour, and it can cover a range of 60 miles.

Tesla is convinced the Cybertruck production equipment will be completed by May 2021, with trial runs commencing before the end of the second quarter of 2021. Unlike the Model 3 and Model Y production lines, the Cybertruck equipment will require less time to organize. It'll have no stamping machine due to its "XY design," and it won't need a paint shop because of the Cybertruck's steel exoskeleton. These advantages will put Tesla on track to begin deliveries of two variants—Tri-Motor AWD and Dual-Motor AWD—in late 2021.

Tesla has three operational Gigafactories, with two more being added in Berlin and Texas. Tesla's first car factory outside of the U.S. is Gigafactory Shanghai, which has now achieved a run rate of 3,000 units per week. This factory was constructed and began production in a mind-boggling timeframe. Within about six months, Tesla went from obtaining permits to electricity hook-up to a brand-new usable facility.

Tesla has gained immense support from the Chinese government because China is already the largest electric vehicle market in the world. This is due in part to China's supportive government policies for electric vehicles. At their Shanghai facility, Tesla plans to manufacture a compact electric car for worldwide consumption. They'll be able to reduce the overall production costs by utilizing locally manufactured parts rather than paying tariffs from U.S. importing. Tesla plans to source 100 percent of its parts locally by the end of 2020.

Musk is convinced the Gigafactory Berlin facility—currently under construction—will surpass the construction speed of the Shanghai facility. Tesla's Berlin factory will have eight "Giga Presses" (casting machines). This means that Tesla will use one large cast to produce vehicles rather than having to assemble multiple parts. This method reduces cost, optimizes vehicle construction, and cuts production time. Not only has Tesla created their own space in the electric vehicle market, but the way they're rapidly changing the entire automotive market is something nobody saw coming—other than Musk himself, of course.

Tesla's Gigafactory Texas is where the much-anticipated Cybertruck will be manufactured. With rough grading commencing on July 17, 2020, to its first usable space expected late December 2020, this means the factory would be partially operational in less than six months—right on track for trial production of the famed Cybertruck in May 2021.

Tesla's stock is widely viewed as a "story stock." This means that its stock doesn't hold much of its value in terms of financial results, but rather its success has everything to do with its "future" pipeline of potential. While the company has endured early production delays, labor cost overruns, and vehicle inefficiencies, they've resiliently benefited from their dominant position in the electric vehicle industry. Although this may be the case, Tesla appears overvalued as it has yet to grow into its financial valuation.

Within the top three results of Google's search engine after typing the words "Should I" is "should I buy a Tesla stock." People aren't 100% sure if they should invest in Tesla stock. However, there have been large amounts of inessential losses and gains due to FOMO (fear of missing out) anxiety alone. Musk has had a controversial impact on the human race, and perhaps this is what he planned the effect to be since Tesla's inception.

After struggling through the first half of 2019 due to doubt over consumer demand, Tesla stock skyrocketed, reporting profits in both the third and fourth quarters of 2019. At the same time, Tesla's market cap grew to more than twice the combined size of rival automakers General Motors and Ford. As of December 2020, Tesla's market cap has topped $600 billion—six months ago, it was celebrating $200 billion. Tesla has come a long way. Musk has a "Giga" vision that has already surpassed what any other automakers have been able to do within such a short period. They've become the largest automaker in the world simply by market capitalization.

Specifically, due to the company's involvement in solar panel installations and energy storage products, Tesla Motors officially became Tesla, Inc. in 2017. Today, Tesla is the parent company to SolarCity, a solar energy initiative that seeks to revolutionize and mainstream solar energy. As such, Tesla is one of the world's leading suppliers of clean alternative energy.

Musk heavily believes the three components essential for a future of viable energy are:

- Producing energy

- Storing energy

- Transferring energy

The high demand for producing renewable energy while having means to store energy in batteries correspond with each other, and it makes complete sense for Tesla to expand its operation in this realm.

Tesla's 2015 launch of the "Powerwall" system is a remarkable feat for the energy industry. This unique lithium-ion rechargeable home battery system allows consumers to save utility costs by maximizing a home's energy self-reliance. During peak energy consumption times, like the evening, Powerwall offers clean energy created and stored during the day. This removes strain on the grid and reduces home utility costs. Tesla distributed its 100,000th Powerwall in early 2020.

While roughly 10% of the U.S. still prefers gas-fired power to renewable energy, Europe looks to embrace renewables with their complete ban on coal-fired power by 2025.

In May 2020, Tesla got the go-ahead for electricity production in the U.K, obtaining its "Electrical Generation License." Tesla is looking to revolutionize the energy market in the U.K. by establishing virtual power plants utilizing its real-time trading and control platform called "Autobidder."

Tesla grew their impact in 2017 with the $66 million installation of the "Powerpack" in Australia—the world's first largest rechargeable lithium-ion battery. Autobidder presently operates in South Australia at

Hornsdale Power Reserve and in its first year reduced the grid service cost by ninety percent or $40 million. This real-time optimized trading platform offers customers self-governing monetization of battery assets to purchase energy at low cost and sell it high.

The "Megapack" launched in 2019. With its interesting capability to store more energy, the Megapack aims to target large electric utility projects like PG&E's Moss Landing, California substation, where Tesla will deploy 256 Megapacks. The entire project will become fully operational by mid-2021. Moss Landing is predicted to save $100 million in the electric utility, and it'll be equivalent to roughly 90,000 Powerwalls.

With Tesla's Gigafactory Berlin increasing the demand for energy in the area, Germany is a prime location Tesla will look to launch its sustainable energy advancement V2G—vehicle-to-grid "smart system on wheels." Musk admits that Tesla's vehicle batteries may soon act as "Powerwalls." This system will allow for the electric vehicles to "control their load" by charging outside of peak energy demand, reducing costs and strain on the grid. Owners will then be able to sell the stored energy back to the grid with a bidirectional charger as demand increases. Tesla has recently commented on bringing this method to the U.K. market as well.

During Battery Day in 2020, we failed to see a battery. All we got were plans for the battery. These include the plan to manufacture a battery by Tesla, the plan to mine their own lithium, and a plan to process and manufacture the raw materials associated with the battery. Most of these plans sounded incredibly impressive as we expect nothing less from the genius Elon Musk. However, many experts suggested that this territory was not for Tesla, and they may be going in it without a sense of clear direction and aim.

Experts suggest that Musk's plan to mine their own lithium is ill-advised. It is an incredibly challenging task, and it is not the same as landing a rocket. Of course, we will only get to know whether they are able to do this once the mining starts. Musk has already secured rights to a lithium clay deposit in Nevada that is spread over ten thousand acres. There is also a cathode manufacturing facility along with the mine, which will add to the network of Tesla's operations and factories in North America.

However, the only problem with this task is that before this, there has never been commercial production of lithium, especially from clay sources. Lithium all over the world comes from only two sources. These include the hard rock deposits in Australia and the brine deposits in Bolivia, Argentina, and Chile. We all know how much Musk likes breaking barriers, so let's see if he is able to break this one by being the first one to commercially produce lithium from a clay source.

The genius engineer is well-aware that this is uncharted territory as he has accepted that himself during Battery Day. Even though lithium companies in Nevada have attempted to mine lithium from clay sources, they have not yet been successful in their ventures. Musk did not give more information during the Battery Day when the mining process will begin, but it is expected to happen shortly if they plan to release a battery by next year.

Another important point to note during Battery Day was that Musk announced he would cut the cost of batteries by more than half. When they achieve this aim, Tesla will be able to produce electric cars at a much lesser cost. In fact, he even promised everyone a $25,000 Tesla electric car within the next three years. Of course, this is not the first time Musk has promised something like this, so we will only have to wait and see.

Besides that, he also announced larger cells to increase energy capacity, novel tabless battery cells, module-less battery packs, battery cells forming the structure of the car, and much more. Musk also said that these are the challenges they soon have to overcome, and they will be able to optimize their battery-making process in the next two years. His vision for the batteries of the future is incredibly bold, but the only problem is that he has not laid out a clear path for its execution (at least he has not made it public – which may well be intentional. One cannot divulge all secrets to the competitors). To a new person, these ideas may seem haphazard without any aim or direction.

Musk's promises have been bold and big, but only time will tell if he is able to fulfill all these promises. Even investors that came to the Battery Day event seemed disappointed and expressed their concerns over what Musk has in his mind. They expressed that Musk has been unrealistic and does not have a clear direction in this plan.

Tesla became a part of the S&P 500 on December 21, 2020. This establishes Tesla as a strong pillar of the automotive, energy, and tech industry

In June 2020, the Chinese government approved Tesla to build new Model 3 cars using a lithium-iron-phosphate battery. With Tesla sourcing Chinese parts and with their ability to dramatically lower battery costs, it'll leave Tesla in prime contention for becoming a staple in Chinese vehicle manufacturing.

Musk's end plan for this battery advancement is to create self-driving electric "robotaxis" that will offer driverless rideshares. He has announced that the vehicles will be functionally ready by the end of 2020, and he wants to have 1 million of them on the road by then. As Musk realizes this dream, Tesla vehicles will increase in value. As value increases, Tesla vehicles will become more expensive. With the flaws that Tesla's autopilot function still presents in 2020, most aren't convinced Musk will have these on the road before the end of 2021.

SpaceX

Founded in 2002 with the bold goals of reducing the cost of space travel and making possible the colonization of Mars, Elon Musk's SpaceX has grown into a leading private aerospace engineering company.

SpaceX continuously paves the way for private space exploration. As the first private company to:

- Send a liquid rocket into orbit

- Launch, orbit, and recover a spacecraft

- Send a spacecraft/crewed spacecraft to the International Space Station

The company is a current leader in space travel, technology, and exploration. But how did the idea for such a bold company emerge? The answer, of course, lies within the brilliant mind of Elon Musk, the "crazy" entrepreneur who wished to send a greenhouse to Mars.

In order to make his Martian dream come true, Musk would go to Russia in search of rockets. To his dismay, he found that the price of purchasing rockets was too steep, and, in Musk-like fashion, decided to create his own rocket-building company. In doing so, he believed he could save 97% of the cost of his rockets while also helping NASA gain funding for future research.

SpaceX currently leads the way in private aerospace innovation. Compared to competitors such as International Launch Services, SpaceX has completed more successful launches and has received billions of dollars in contract revenue.

With the company's success come a number of landmark achievements that have helped define SpaceX and carve its role as a leader in private space exploration. A few of these achievements include the first relaunch and landing of a used orbital rocket stage (accomplished March 30, 2017) and the first re-flight of a commercial cargo spacecraft (accomplished on June 3, 2017).

Since 2008, SpaceX has partnered with NASA to send spacecraft to the ISS. In 2012, SpaceX became the first commercial company to deliver cargo to the International Space Station (ISS) using a Crew Dragon reusable capsule and the Falcon 9 rocket. Since their groundbreaking achievement in 2012, SpaceX has delivered cargo to the ISS around two dozen times. What's really exciting, though, is that the same Capsule brought Bob Behnken and Doug Hurley—two veteran astronauts—to the ISS during the crewed Demo-2 test mission on May 30, 2020. Demo-2 was completed when Bob and Doug landed back on Earth on August 2, 2020. The mission marks the culmination of a partnership with NASA, which has been unable to fly from US soil since retiring its fleet in 2011. While the Crew Dragon capsule had visited the ISS during the unmanned Demo-1 test flight in March 2019, this was the first time a SpaceX spacecraft had taken a crew into space. The future of this will be to carry private passengers into space, knocking manned space travel off the list of feats.

Like any of Musk's other entrepreneurial endeavors, it's quickly becoming clear that his vision of the commercial space industry is the future.

Falcon 9 has launched into space over 90 times with 94 full mission completions. However, Musk is no stranger to bouncing back from failures. Two failures from Falcon 9 first stage operations are:

SpaceX crashed multiple boosters in failed landing attempts prior to landing the first stage of an orbital-class rocket in 2015.

In June 2018, one of their spacecraft exploded mid-flight.

The Falcon 9 is the world's first orbital-class rocket capable of re-flight. The rocket is comprised of two stages. SpaceX has re-flown stage one of its rockets roughly thirty-eight times to date. It's designed specifically around transporting cargo *and* people beyond Earth's orbit. Falcon 9 can carry a maximum of 50,300 pounds or 22,800 kilograms. Musk confirms that reusable rockets can reduce costs and enhance efficiency within the aerospace industry. Costs of space travel are heavily reduced because the most expensive parts of the rocket can be reused. Therefore, more access to space exploration is possible.

The launch price of Falcon 9 was estimated to be $57 million in 2012. Today, a Falcon 9 launch costs $62 million. Missions in general cost 4% to insure. A typical mission from competitors like Arianespace runs upward of $165 million, which costs them just under $7 million in insurance premiums. SpaceX missions are only around $2.5 million in premiums.

When SpaceX re-uses parts of its rockets, it can charge less than its list price. The first stage boosters make up roughly sixty percent of the total cost of rockets—$37 million. Rockets' nosecones make up about ten percent or $6 million of the total cost. Sometimes, SpaceX will go as far as fishing the nosecones out of the ocean or retrieve them with nets. SpaceX can keep the method to their madness secretive because they're a private company. Predictions show that SpaceX can bring the price of launches down to below $30 million per launch, which is unparalleled.

On February 6, 2018, SpaceX set the bar even higher. To no surprise, Musk is responsible for creating the world's most powerful rocket by a factor of two—the Falcon Heavy. This reusable rocket has twenty-seven Merlin engines on its first stage, which are capable of more than five million pounds of force of thrust at liftoff. With only a handful of launches and re-flown rockets thus far, Falcon Heavy is already respected in the industry as being the most capable rocket flying today. Leave it to Musk once again to entirely disrupt another field of interest.

The Crew Dragon missions are an essential part of SpaceX. The first launch of the Crew Dragon capsule to the ISS happened on March 2, 2019. The flight was known as Demo-1, and this was a five-day mission. Demo-1's mission was to test the equipment of the Crew Dragon and its systems. The capsule came back after completing the mission successfully, and then it was time for Demo-2.

Demo-2 was the second part of the testing phase and a part of NASA's Commercial Crew Program. The spacecraft lifted off from Florida from a Falcon 9 rocket. The flight was a test to certify if SpaceX's system can be utilized to regularly take a crew to and from the ISS. The flight was a huge success and has given hope to SpaceX for tourist flights in late 2021.

After the success of both these flights, it was time for the Crew-1 mission. On November 16, 2020, the Crew Dragon docked at the ISS. Four astronauts have left for a six-month mission to the ISS. They plan to undock in May 2021, so we will have to wait and see its result next year. We are hoping the mission will be as successful as Demo 1 and Demo 2.

Assuming the success of Crew-1 and no major problems are discovered during the reviewing of data from the Demo-2 mission, NASA will at this point endorse SpaceX's rocket and capsule system to fly astronauts to the ISS regularly. Musk simply keeps reaching new heights with his quite literally out-of-this-world imagination.

SpaceX isn't going to pursue the human-rating certification for Falcon spacecraft to transport NASA astronauts. Instead, the Starship launch system will replace the Falcon spacecraft family.

The Starship transportation system is SpaceX's "fully re-usable, two-stage-to-orbit, super heavy-lift launch vehicle," which has been in development since 2012. The "Starship" itself is the second stage of the vehicle. Designed to carry its crew, passengers, and cargo to Earth's orbit and beyond, it's the most powerful space launch vehicle ever produced. It's designed to deliver satellites further and at a lower cost than the Falcon crafts. There are plans to have the Starship bring humans to Mars and transport the largest space telescopes known to man. The first test flights for Starship prototypes commenced in July 2019, and construction on its launch mount is underway.

More than nine prototypes of the Starship have been built as of December 2020. The first two prototypes were destroyed during pressure tests in November 2019 and February 2020. Another prototype collapsed during testing a month later, and one more blew up during a test in May 2020. On December 9, 2020, Starship prototype SN8 performed the first high-altitude (12.5 km) test flight, executing a successful skydiver-like descent using high-drag body flaps, followed by a reorientation burn and propulsive landing in the center of the landing area. The hard landing was a result of lower-than-expected pressure in the methane header tank, resulting in the vehicle exploding on the landing pad.

During SpaceX's eleventh mission of 2020, they ferried a next-generation GPS satellite, the GPS III SV03, into orbit for the U.S. Space Force. These upgraded systems are three times more accurate than their predecessors, and it appears SpaceX will take on the extraordinary role of transporting more of these in the future. There are currently three global positioning systems like this one in orbit.

The goal of reaching Mars is to search for water and build a propellant plant that would aid future missions. To further aid in this endeavor, Musk aims to send four more spacecraft to the red planet by 2024 to begin the process of colonization. SpaceX's first private passenger will be Japanese entrepreneur Yusaku Maezawa, and he'll fly around the Moon within one week in 2023. This mission will specifically help SpaceX fund developments toward Starship and its forerunner Super Heavy—a proof of concept.

It seems as if all is going to plan for Musk and crew, as the 2024 timeline set for colonization of Mars slowly arrives. With SpaceX, the "real-life Tony Stark" is having the time of his life—and perhaps paving the way for the future of manned interplanetary travel in the process.

Starlink

On December 18, 2018, SpaceX raised $500 million to fund an enormous satellite internet project—Starlink. The capital came mostly from existing shareholders. Before anyone even really knew what Starlink was, the company's estimated 2025 valuation was already a whopping $30.5 billion.

Musk's plan with Starlink is to build its own constellation of roughly 12,000 compact mass-produced satellites in low Earth orbit (LEO). In late 2019, the Federal Communications Commission (FCC) submitted filings to the International Telecommunication Union (ITU) on behalf of SpaceX to arrange a spectrum for 30,000 additional Starlink satellites to supplement the 12,000 Starlink satellites already approved by the FCC. The company is currently constructing a system of ground stations and user terminals that'll connect users directly to its wireless network. This system will provide broadband speeds similar to those of fiber optic networks.

Product development for the company began in 2015, and the first two prototype test satellites were launched in February 2018. The second set of test satellites took flight in May 2019, and the first sixty functional satellites were also launched at this time.

In just over two years, SpaceX has launched 775 Starlink satellites into space with intentions to launch up to sixty more on each Falcon 9 flight going forward. These launches take place as often as every two weeks. Musk plans to have 2,000 Starlink satellites in orbit by 2021, and with 775 satellites already launched, this once aggressive timeline doesn't seem so aggressive at all now. At least 800 satellites have to be deployed for the system to become operational. Musk plans to mass-produce the compact satellites at a lower cost and higher speed of production.

Starlink has made unprecedented progress with the development of this satellite project. Previously, Iridium held the record for the largest commercial satellite constellation, and they were launching about six satellites per month. SpaceX currently carries sixty on one flight every two weeks, and with plans to bring its Starship launch vehicle online sooner than later, each flight will be able to transport 400 Starlink satellites.

Around 700,000 people across the U.S. alone have shown interest in the Starlink internet service. This has caused SpaceX to increase their initial request for user terminals to the FCC from 1 million to 5 million.

SpaceX announced a new SmallSat Rideshare Mission program in August 2019. This program will accommodate an adaptable, feasible transportation method for smaller satellite operators to reach orbit. An online booking system through SpaceX's website has already received more than 100 reservations. One trip to orbit costs $1 million, and the Falcon 9 will be used to ferry payloads to multiple orbits from a single launch.

As of 2020, about forty percent of the world doesn't have steady internet access. Musk's end goal is to allow the entire globe access to affordable internet. We must remember that as we experience nearly half of the world's population join the digital world by 2021, the makeup of digital culture will alter significantly—as if Musk hasn't thought about his next venture to solve this potential issue already.

SolarCity

Founded in 2006 by brothers Peter and Lyndon Rive, SolarCity was born to revolutionize solar energy production. The idea for the company was floated by the brothers' cousin, Elon Musk; after only three years of operation, the company had supplied solar panels to thousands of homes that were generating 440 megawatts of power.

As the company continued to grow, it acquired rival companies groSolar and Clean Currents. The expansion allowed the company, which was based in California, to move eastward. The brothers opened a second SolarCity in Connecticut.

The move proved useful. Just seven short years after starting their California-based venture, the brothers reined over the leading residential solar panel installer in the United States. This growth allowed the company to purchase Paramount Solar for $120 million later in 2013. Using this as a launching point, SolarCity began to install solar panels rapidly, with installation rates for 2015 equaling nearly 30% of all solar panel installation in the United States.

In June 2016, the company was purchased by Tesla Motors for a price of $2.6 billion. Following the acquisition, Tesla became the parent company for SolarCity, and Elon Musk was instated as company chairman. Consequently, Musk began to use SolarCity as a means to grow his Tesla company into a leading solar energy producer.

Through SolarCity, Musk makes solar panels, roofs, tiles, and batteries supplied by his Tesla brand. Many of these products are designed for cutting edge and work hand in hand with Tesla vehicles to provide a cleaner automotive experience.

However, some see ulterior motives behind Tesla's acquisition of SolarCity, a company that had been rapidly losing stock value and accruing debt since its 2014 heyday. Critics view Musk's acquisition as an attempt to save his cousins' business—fine, perhaps, but a definite rebuild, for sure. In fact, there's no way to deny the fact that in acquiring SolarCity, Tesla found itself hands-on with a company in free fall.

Time will tell if the Tesla-SolarCity merger were foolhardy or a brilliant move. As of now, however, it seems that Musk has largely been able to stop the bleeding. It will be interesting to see how Musk handles the situation moving forward. The engineer-entrepreneur has already overseen a direction of SolarCity products to be used in the production of Tesla brands, a move that's helped close up the wound that was SolarCity.

Musk hopes to turn SolarCity's fortunes upside down and, by doing so, increase the efficiency of his Tesla models. This will also enable the growth of the Tesla brand and further expansion as the dominant electric automobile retailer.

The Boring Company

It turns out that Musk isn't only invested in making interplanetary travel easier. Instead, the entrepreneur is also focused on making travel more convenient and a little closer to home.

You may be surprised at his unconventional approach, however. While many genius engineers dream of flying cars and teleportation systems, Musk has his eyes set on tunnel boring. With underground 3D tunnels, Musk hopes to develop a transportation system that eliminates congestion and provides extra benefits to the commuter.

Enter the Boring Company, a December 2016 invention by Elon Musk. According to Musk, the Boring company will aid in developing the future of transportation. The genius understands that responses to his idea will be mixed.

Why tunnels?

That's the million-dollar question and one that Musk answers in detail on his company website. A look at the company's FAQ provides the following information:

- Tunnels can be built in multiple layers, meaning there's no congestion—ever

- Tunnels aren't subject to weather delays or hazards

- Tunnel construction is silent and invisible

- Tunnels bring communities closer together by removing large barriers

If Musk's vision is to be realized, however, it will come only after significant strides. According to the data, the current costs of tunnel digging can exceed $1 billion per mile. The Boring Company seeks to reduce the cost of boring by a factor of at least ten.

The Boring Company looks to reduce boring costs in a couple of ways:

- Reduce Tunnel Diameter—By reducing tunnel diameter from twenty-eight to fourteen feet, boring costs can be reduced by up to 4 times the original amount.

- Improve Tunnel Boring Machine Speeds—Tunnel boring is expensive because it's slow. Musk's company seeks to increase tunnel speed, power, and efficiency to significantly reduce tunnel boring costs.

While this in itself appears quite a tall order, Musk's vision of a tunnel transportation system doesn't stop there. In fact, the serial entrepreneur has dreams of using these tunnels to propel his Hyperloop transportation system into reality.

What's the Hyperloop, you ask? Simply put, it's a revolutionary mode of transportation designed by Musk and still in its theoretical stage. The Hyperloop seeks to place passenger or freight trains into an air-tight vacuum. Trains would levitate off the ground through the power of magnetism; this, plus the vacuum tube surrounding the train, would allow the vehicle to move without friction.

According to Musk, the Hyperloop will move at the speed of sound. And that's just a minimum.

With goals so large, it's no wonder the visionary entrepreneur has created his own boring company to improve tunnel infrastructure. While the Boring Company is still in its infancy, it's already begun to make significant strides toward its goals.

With significant portions of the tunnel already dug at Musk's SpaceX property, testing is already underway for the genius's pet project—a tunnel that will go from LAX to Culver City, further to Santa Monica, and terminating in Westwood. This route will be the home to a new mode of transportation that will see cars transported on electric sleds at 120mph. According to Musk, this will reduce transportation time from forty-five minutes to five minutes.

Think that's exciting? Musk boasts of government approval to construct a Hyperloop tunnel that will connect the cities of New York, Philadelphia, Baltimore, and Washington, D.C. Musk's vision would take people between D.C. and Baltimore in fifteen minutes. With multiple permits already in place, it appears the genius engineer's dream could be realized sooner than any of us think.

The Boring Company possesses two tunnel boring machines (TBMs) with a third on the way, each named after a work of art. In order, the TBMs are referred to as *"Godot, "Line-storm,"* and *"Prufrock."* The final, Prufrock, has been in development since May of 2018. Prototypes of this model show that this TBM could be the fastest ever developed— up to ten times the speed of standard TBMs.

Musk claims The Boring Company can allow for tunneling to be fifteen times faster and ten times cheaper. If successful, this TBM model could help pave the way for the future of American transportation infrastructure.

As of December 2020, the proposed Hyperloops between Washington D.C. and Baltimore and between D.C. and New York are both on hold. The Baltimore link is under environmental review, and the New York link is being questioned as to whether or not Musk has adequate approvals to complete the project.

A second Hyperloop tunnel project was planned in Chicago to connect passengers to the Airport, and The Boring Company was selected to construct it by then-mayor Rahm Emanuel. When a new mayor, Lori Lightfoot, got appointed into office in May 2019, this high-speed project was squashed. She didn't believe he could build it without any city money, and she didn't see the need for this particular method of transportation. To no surprise, Musk didn't let this "no" stop him from pursuing his interest in boring.

The first outside funds to come into The Boring Company came in July 2019 when Musk sold $120 million of the company's stock to Venture Capital investors, and he saw a $920 million valuation. The new capital more than doubled the number of funds brought in from the tunneling startup thus far. Although, out of the $113 million raised last year, ninety percent of that was Musk's investment. Musk also sold merchandise like the unforgettable flamethrowers—bringing in $10 million of capital in 100 hours—to fund The Boring Company.

Musk has since scrapped the 2017 plan to construct the tunnel under Los Angeles. This came after a number of groups sued the city of L.A. over it as residents were frustrated to see Musk's plan be exempt from the environmental reviews. The Boring Company decided to look into constructing a tunnel at Los Angeles Dodgers Stadium instead.

Named the "Dugout Loop"—pun definitely intended—this 3-mile single underground tunnel will shuttle fans from subway lines to the Dodgers baseball stadium within four minutes. It'll operate at high speeds of 125 and 150 miles per hour with zero emissions between Los Feliz, East Hollywood, or Rampart Village neighborhoods and Dodger Stadium in the City of Los Angeles.

Two benefits of this project:

The Boring Project doesn't need to raise capital for the Dugout Loop. The company plans to pay for the project out of its own pocket.

The suggested route travels strictly below property already owned by The Boring Company and public land.

The anticipated completion of the Dugout Loop was supposed to be in time for the 2020 baseball season. Shortly after this announcement, the company won a high-profile bid to build a "Loop" tunnel system under Las Vegas. The "Dugout Loop" has since taken a back seat. Now, with coronavirus in the forefront and the project sitting under environmental review, it's uncertain when The Boring Company will be able to revisit the project.

What started initially as a joke due to Musk's frustrations toward congestion of vehicle traffic on the streets of Los Angeles, his idea is respectfully becoming a revolutionary method of transportation.

The "LVCC Loop" in Las Vegas—the first Boring Company project to be completed—will consist of two tunnels for vehicles, three stations, and it'll have a pedestrian tunnel. This system will begin at the Las Vegas Convention Centre. In August, designs were approved for two additional tunnels that'll connect hotels with the Convention Centre. Resorts World Hotel is one of the hotels confirmed to be connecting to the "Loop," and the expansion is set to begin by the end of 2020. Tests of the tunnel will begin by November. It's undecided what kind of vehicle will move through the Las Vegas tunnel, but Model X, Model 3, or electric vehicles with a sixteen-person tram are all being taken into consideration.

There have been recent conversations between Airport personnel and The Boring Company. With the "LVCC Loop" already near completion with approved expansions and a potential tunnel between the Airport and Las Vegas Boulevard, Elon Musk is well on his way to becoming a predominant figure of Las Vegas transportation. It's even rumored Musk is keeping quiet about a possible tunnel between Adelanto, California, and Las Vegas.

It seems like Musk is on to something. Musk believes he can transform the way—and the speed, of course—people are shuttled to and from major airports. The Boring Company's $45-$60 million proposal for the "Rancho Cucamonga-Ontario Airport" tunnel will be 35 feet underground, 2.8 miles long, and 14 feet in diameter. They'll use electric vans that seat 12 people at one time—designed by Tesla, of course—and they'll travel up to 127 miles per hour. The Ontario Airport Loop in San Bernardino County, CA, is expected to be completed in four years.

Although the cost of the project could slightly exceed $60 million, this is still substantially less than light-rail, which could run costs of up to $1.5 billion, and they often take up to ten years to complete.

The Boring Company has still only one fully completed tunnel to date: The Test Tunnel at the SpaceX parking lot. Despite this, Musk has already made boring more efficient. He's tripled the amount of power entering the TBMs, and he's heightened the intricacies of the cooling systems. The TBMs have been modified to allow for the machine to work while the team erects supports.

More boring machine enhancements include:

Modified cutter design to ensure better efficiency.

An automated erection system so that the machine can help cut down on labor and time.

The Boring Company hasn't yet been able to see how quickly the newly modified boring machines can work due to the Las Vegas project being focused more on quality than accelerated digging time. When the time comes, though, these machines are bound to raise the boring bar.

With the growing interest in Musk's unique tunneling systems, could we perhaps see Musk taking The Boring Company into international markets? Something would make one believe that Musk is already a step ahead of these thoughts.

OpenAI

OpenAI is a non-profit, San Francisco-based research organization that focuses on developing friendly and human-compatible AI systems that can benefit mankind in a positive way. Founded by Elon Musk, the organization seeks to collaborate with other institutions for the advancement of AI technologies and systems.

OpenAI was formed in October 2015 by Elon Musk and Sam Altman. Along with other investors, the two pledged over $1 billion to the organization, which is expected to grow in the coming years. According to reports, the company was founded in part to combat the advancement of "super intelligent" AI systems, which both Musk and Altman view as a danger to the human race. In doing so, Musk hopes that the research gained from OpenAI can be used to promote a safer technological landscape.

OpenAI's first major service, Universe, was released in December 2016 and is aimed at measuring and training general AI intelligence across a variety of platforms. The platform is a valuable research tool that gives developers a greater idea of different AI systems and the intelligence levels they hold.

In February 2018, Musk resigned from the company on the grounds that his involvement could be a conflict of interest with his Tesla AI development. Despite this, the genius remains committed to the cause and is a major financial backer.

OpenAI looks at the growth of AI systems through deep learning technology. This form of AI computing looks to provide machines with general patterns that can be turned into multiple algorithms. This provides computers with boundless knowledge compared to the hand-plugged algorithms of just a few years prior. With deep learning, systems are finally beginning to take shape on their own—a thought that has both positive and negative implications.

Through the development of friendly AI systems, OpenAI hopes to develop positive technological structures that will benefit the human race and not lead to harmful superintelligence. Already, as the organization states on their website, artificial intelligence has learned how to be "creative," how-to "dream," and how to "experience the world."

Musk, a staunch opponent to AI superintelligence, hopes that OpenAI can combat potential Terminator-like situations. While the jury is still out on the development and feasibility of artificial intelligence systems that could surpass human knowledge and capabilities, Musk believes that OpenAI is more a necessity than a desire.

In other words, this is the total opposite of the Founder, CEO, and Lead Designer of SpaceX's lavish colonization of Mars. As part of OpenAI's mission statement, the organization emphasizes its non-profit status. This status, it claims, bears witness to the company's commitment to developing AI systems that will have a "positive human impact."

OpenAI's non-profit status provides other benefits, as well. Because the organization is not beholden to corporate interests, it can focus solely on the development of AI systems and technological growth. What's more, its free communication and collaboration policy shows that the organization sacrifices nothing when it comes to developing effective AI systems.

The future of Musk's OpenAI is yet to be written. Still, with Musk's strong support, it's likely that this valuable non-profit will be making headlines for years to come.

Neuralink

Imagine a world where humans and androids collide. In this world, superhuman figures with access to an unfathomable amount of knowledge battle it out with advanced AI systems that have gotten too smart for the good of humanity.

Sound like science fiction?

Not to Elon Musk. To the genius, who desperately wishes to remove the existential threat of superintelligent AI, this type of AI-enhanced human, or transhuman, might be the only way to save the human race.

That's why Musk formed Neuralink in 2016. This highly secretive company seeks to develop implantable brain-computer interfaces (BCIs) that can be inserted into a human's brain and allow them superhuman capabilities.

I know what you're thinking—that sounds pretty awesome.

Musk reportedly got the idea from Iain M Banks' *The Culture*, which uses a concept known as "neural lace" to achieve symbiosis with artificial intelligence. This connection would allow humans access to a range of knowledge and information previously not accessible to man.

In an interview discussing AI, Neuralink founder Elon Musk stated that, despite critic backlash, artificial intelligence is dangerously close to outsmarting the human race. As such, it's no wonder that the entrepreneur would keep his Neuralink project under wraps.

It goes without saying that the company does not follow OpenAI's free collaboration policies. Despite this, a quick visit to the Neuralink website shows that the company is hiring quality scientists and engineers from a variety of fields. Prior experience in neurotechnology, the website states, is not required. In fact, the company is expecting most of its workers to come from other fields.

In a September 2018 interview with Joe Rogan, Musk stated that Neuralink would be announcing a new product in a few months. The product, aimed at seamlessly connecting humans with AI, will be, according to Musk, "…better than anyone thinks."

Asked who could use the product, Musk responded, "It will enable anyone who wants to have superhuman cognition."

It's worth wondering, then, if the genius himself has already achieved this advanced state of cognition. With Tesla sales advancing like never before and his status as a cultural and scientific icon steadily growing, it certainly seems like the eccentric visionary knows all the answers.

Within one-year, Neuralink received an FDA Breakthrough Device designation in July of 2020 and is currently preparing for the first human implantation. Of course, that will take time as now the implantations in pigs are being perfected.

Neuralink's generalized brain device has evolved greatly in just one year. The first prototype consisted of multiple parts—one that sat behind one's ear with wires being traced to the brain—big and tacky. As of November 2020, the device is much simpler. It's wireless, and it's as small as a large coin. The device, Link V0.9, is invisible to the human eye once it's implanted into the skull. Musk hopes that this device will be able to restore brain functions in people with various disorders such as insomnia, seizures, blindness, memory loss, deafness, blindness, paraplegia, quadriplegia, etc.

The tiny device replaces a piece of skull, and the wires connect to the low-level cortex (superficial part of the brain) not far from the device itself. V0.9 is designed to identify and transmit patterns of neural activity. Musk says, "it's like a FitBit in your skull with tiny wires." The device's battery lasts all day, and it charges inductively like your typical cell phone.

Neuralink is aiming to pursue the first implants of the compact device in the skulls of quadriplegics. There are no other treatments available to people with quadriplegia other than using a brain implant to control a robotic arm, so getting approval for this human experiment is relatively easy.

If we're able to sense what someone wants to do with their limbs, a second device can be implanted to create a "neuro shunt" to redirect neurons throughout the body. With the amount of science that can be condensed into bite-sized architecture, a superhuman future doesn't seem so science fiction after all, does it?

Musk always knew something like the V0.9 could become a reality, but he also knew it could solve real-life issues. The link can monitor the health and warn wearers of heart attacks or strokes, for example. In real-time, it can measure temperature, pressure, etc. Funny enough, this little device could even play music if you so desired.

V0.9 will be, according to Musk, quite pricey when it first launches. However, the cost will dramatically decrease over time. They're aiming for a price point of around U.S. $3,000, similar to what the cost of laser eye surgery is now. Neuralink's brain device uses a lot of parts that are in smartphones, watches, etc., so it's not all that expensive to produce them on a mass scale.

The surgery to implant V0.9 takes less than an hour—leaving the hospital the same day—and there's no need for general anesthesia. Robots have been designed to automate the surgical process, removing the potential for human error. The robot images the brain to ensure no damage to veins or arteries occurs. The operation is also reversible, and the device can be removed.

Currently, there is available technology—the Utah Array—already in use. The device has been implanted in a handful of people, but it's very prone to causing brain injury and infection because of stiff electrodes. Also, it is conspicuous due to its little tiny boxes sticking out of the head.

Although this isn't the most effective method, it works. It's a valuable proof of concept for Musk.

Deep Brain Stimulation is another technology that's currently available. However, this method offers more disadvantages than it does benefits. Although this current technology has helped over 150,000 people, it isn't always guaranteed to work. Over time, Deep Brain Stimulation destroys brain matter, and it doesn't read or write high-bandwidth information.

Simply put, Musk's technology is science and tech mastery compressed into one device. It will pioneer the way we analyze brain activity. It's not like he hasn't done this before in other markets, and this is why Neuralink is worth looking out for.

Neuralink chose to test V0.9 on pigs, as pigs share very similar anatomy with humans, specifically our skulls. To test the device, Musk's team at Neuralink embedded the device into Gertrude the pig's skull with the fine wires touching her brain. The electrodes were capable of sensing, documenting, and in a way revitalizing brain activity. Gertrude also walked on a treadmill as a study to show how effective the device is at reading brain activity. Through this experiment, the team was able to correctly depict the positions of her limbs while in motion. Neuralink's implanted device left Gertrude with no wires sticking out of her skin, which means there is no chance of infection. These results reassure safe testing on animals.

A second pig had the device implanted into her skull and then removed successfully without any health repercussions. She was as happy as she was prior to the implant and also while wearing the implant. There was no change in the pig's behavior at any stage of testing whatsoever.

Not only do these tests prove that the device is safe and doesn't change behavior, but testing this particular device without wires sticking out of the skin may also revitalize the animal testing industry's dwindling reputation. Infections in animals would be greatly reduced, allowing testing on animals to be a safe practice. Neuralink has since been applauded by industry professionals for paying attention to the morals of animal testing procedures. Consequently, improved animal testing methods means improved research in humans.

Neuralink performs all work on the device in-house, which allows them to ensure the utmost security and authenticity of their product. Data captured from the brain will be encrypted and authenticated, and because Neuralink builds the device from the ground up, this gives their team ample opportunity to embed security into the design.

Having detailed resources in-house also allows them to physically test the device against elements it'll be exposed to once implanted into the skull, such as bodily chemicals, tissue growing over it, fluids, etc. They test its overall robustness by mimicking the conditions the devices will see while implanted in the body.

The future of Neuralink is very bright. Needless to say, Musk is well on his way to revolutionizing health technology, all while improving testing on animals.

Today, Neuralink is focused on implanting into the low-level cortex because as they develop the product, this simplifies problems they may encounter with going deeper into the human brain. A lot of human responses happen in the low-level cortex. Even at the surface, Neuralink is certain their technology will allow for the movement of limbs, and it'll at least cure deafness and blindness.

Musk believes that comprehensive technology implantations like V0.9 will evolve into new opportunities like retina prosthetics. Somewhere down the line, Neuralink predicts they'll be able to plug a camera right into the visual cortex. It's also believed that Neuralink's future may offer "super-vision," where people will be able to see with ultra-violet or infrared vision. Musk says, "the future's going to be weird."

To save and replay memories and download them into another body or robot is also on the list of Neuralink's many achievable notions. Another extremely fascinating future capability of their technology will be to compress thoughts into words. To us, telepathy may be mind-boggling, but Musk says a function like this is well within reach. He believes Neuralink will create a device, if not upgrades to this one, that will remove the energy involved with transforming thoughts into words. Conveying uncompressed thoughts to someone else will result in better communication globally.

The only difference V0.9 needs to dig past the low-level cortex into the hypothalamus is the length of the electrodes—a very simple adjustment. The robot used to implant the device is already built to offer implantation of 7cm deep, deeper than what is needed for the wires to be fanned out to the hypothalamus. Although Neuralink is primarily focused on implantation at the low-level cortex, for now, this isn't going to stop them from exploring this type of testing to treat emotional disorders like depression, addiction, and anxiety. Neuralink is only just touching the surface of what their life-changing device is fully capable of.

Over time, they'll capture information from the brain that will enhance their products. It could be said that companies should adapt to technology, but Neuralink doesn't need to adapt—*they* are the technology.

Neuralink's team currently consists of about 100 employees. Musk says he'd like to see it grow to 10,000 or more employees over time. Imagine how 10,000 driven individuals can impact a tiny but monstrous piece of our future.

With cognition at the forefront for Neuralink, they're more than capable of creating a movement in this market that right now seems unparalleled.

The Bottom Line

There's no one quite like Elon Musk.

Whether you call him Tony Stark or simply call him crazy, there's no denying that the genius engineer-entrepreneur is at the forefront of technological innovation and discovery. With successful businesses in a variety of fields, Musk is one of the most accomplished men on Earth.

And he doesn't appear to be slowing down any time soon. With some of his most important and daring ventures in stages of infancy, Musk could be sitting on a technological and financial boom. If the genius entrepreneur's plans come to fruition, the world may look very different in fifty years.

Trains that move at hyper-speed. Cyborgs who can harness the power of AI to gain superhuman knowledge. Tunnels that connect major cities and speed up transportation tenfold.

These sites won't be uncommon if Elon Musk gets his way. With concrete steps in place to realize these efforts, the genius could soon usher in a technological revolution like we've never seen before.

One thing's for sure: with Elon Musk, the future is bound to be a little more interesting.

CHAPTER THREE

ELON MUSK'S FAMILY MEMBERS

While Elon Musk has had a wild life filled with lots of exciting things going on, you will find that he is not the only one in the Musk family to achieve fame. The extent of his fame might be exponentially greater, but there are prominent members of his family who have gained the interest of the public because of the noticeable things they have done. You may or may not have heard of them in connection to the genius himself. Since they are closely linked to the genius entrepreneur, there is more possibility of them turning out to be a muskmelon than anyone else. Let's take a look at the closest family members of Elon Musk and how they live their lives.

The Parents

Before we go on to anyone else, we ought to talk about Musk's parents. These were the individuals that brought the Founder, CEO, and lead designer of SpaceX into this world. While it may seem like Musk's parents must have had an amazing relationship, it was quite the opposite. It is reported that Musk's father was abusive, and his mother went on to file a divorce and took the three children away from his influence. There is a lot of detail regarding this as Musk's mother has gone on record to call his father abusive. Let's take a closer look at the parents of the genius entrepreneur and how they would have impacted his life.

Errol Musk

Let's talk about Musk's father, Musk senior, Errol Musk. He is a renowned engineer and has a genius-level IQ, according to various sources. This can be proven by the fact that he was able to obtain an engineer's qualification at a very young age. It was quite a phenomenal achievement, and we can understand where Elon Musk might get his intelligence from. Even the *Rolling Stone* profile on his father in 2017 acknowledges this.

While Musk went on to live with his father sometime after his parents divorced, he doesn't seem to have fond memories of him. His father actively worked in construction and emerald mining during the time that Musk lived with him.

He might have gotten the intelligence from him, but he surely hasn't left a fatherly impression on him. This was mostly because of incidents similar to the one in 2018 when Errol Musk became notorious for having a child with his stepdaughter. This was something that was denounced by people everywhere, and it made for a very surprising headline.

According to the details that Musk has provided, Errol Musk has done every crime that one might possibly think of. This makes you question a lot of things. So, basically, Musk doesn't have good memories associated with his father.

Maye Musk

Next, we have Mother Musk, namely, Maye Musk. Musk's mother has been in the media ever since she was fifteen when her modeling career started. Not only has she walked down the ramp of New York Fashion Week countless times, but she has also featured on the cereal boxes of Special K and other brilliant platforms. Moreover, she has gone on to feature on the cover of Time magazine.

Her journey as a model didn't stop at an early age. She continues to be featured in various projects. Her latest achievement was in 2017, when she became the spokesperson for Cover Girl. She was aged 69 at that time. All these details surely make us believe that she has made it as a model in her time, and she continues to prove herself till today. The apple didn't fall far from the tree. While Elon Musk's achievements are in an extremely different industry, both of them can be seen to strive for the best.

During the time that she was married to her former husband and Musk's father, Errol Musk, she has deemed it as highly abusive. She sought a divorce from this abusive relationship in 1979 and went on to establish herself in Canada. She, along with three of her children, went on to live a more peaceful life there as she started her practice as a dietician. While Elon Musk lived with her for a while, he soon left to live with his father later.

Elon Musk's Siblings

Musk's parents had three children in total, including him. These included two sons, Elon and Kimbal, and a daughter, Tosca. Musk is the eldest of his siblings and proves to be a great source of inspiration to them and others. Following in the footsteps, the siblings have also come a long way and have established themselves in different ways.

Kimbal Musk

Kimbal Musk, Musk's younger brother, was born on September 20, 1972. It's clear with Kimbal's achievements that the entrepreneurial element runs in the family. He has gone on to establish three real-food businesses that come under the Kitchen Restaurant Group. The companies include Next Door, The Kitchen, and Hedge Row.

The main idea of these companies is to provide access to real food to the masses. Starting from the roots, he offers his services to farmers and goes on to serve real food at every price point available. Not only is he looking for monetary gains, but he has also established a non-profit organization called Big Greens.

All his achievements have led the entrepreneur to be titled the Global Social Entrepreneur. This title was presented to him by the World Economic Forum (WEC). These are surely some great achievements by the talented brother of Elon Musk.

Kimbal is also a proud board member of Tesla and SpaceX. His portfolio has no bounds. He actively supports his older brother with his achievements. They have also gone on to co-found a company called Zip2.

Tosca Musk

Now, we have Musk's younger sister, Tosca Musk. Each of the siblings of the Musk family has their own establishments and achievements. Tosca Musk is fueled by creativity and is passionate when it comes to her media representation. The younger sister of Musk is a devoted filmmaker and has entrepreneurial claims. This comes to show that each family member is loaded with ambition and entrepreneurial skills.

Born in July 1974, the South African filmmaker has come a long way. Each of the siblings ventured out in different directions. Elon went on to excel in the tech industry, Kimbal established himself in the restaurant industry, and Tosca went on to pursue her filmmaking dreams. There were clearly no restrictions on any of the children about what they were required to do in their lives.

Tosca Musk went on to establish her own streaming platform where people can watch original movies and shows. They're mainly based on romance novels. The platform has been quite a hit amongst the viewers. The startup isn't old at all, as it went on to raise about $4.75 million in 2017 as seed funding. That has to say something about her achievements. You won't find just any business acquiring such large capital during seed funding.

Elon Musk's Cousins

Throughout his childhood, as he was growing up, Musk was not only around his siblings, but his cousins played a major part in his upbringing. He spent most of his time surrounded by them. So, it's only normal to include them in his family list. You might think that the Musk siblings were the only ones with the entrepreneurial drive. But that's not all.

Even the cousins of the genius entrepreneur have come a long way and established themselves in different fields. Let's take a look at these astounding individuals who are or can also be seen as muskmelons.

Lyndon Rive

When you think of the Musk family, you believe that they're going to be extremely talented. You're not wrong at this point. Lyndon Rive, born in 1977, is another one of the geniuses who cofounded *SolarCity* back in 2006. This one brings quite the achievement for Musk's cousin.

With a focus on energy-efficiency models, he managed to build a great company, of which he was the CEO till 2017. Tesla acquired the company for an astounding $2.6 billion. While Rive did not have the CEO position after this, he still managed to stay on as head of sales for the energy department of Tesla.

Earlier on, before the establishment of *SolarCity*, Rive and his brothers started another company. This was called *Everdream*. They went on to work for their company for about eight years before selling it to *Dell*. This clearly shows that the entrepreneurial side of the family doesn't stop at the siblings. It goes over and beyond to the cousins as well. Lyndon Rive is one example. There are more cousins of Elon Musk that have made their mark.

Peter Rive

Peter Rive, the brother of Lyndon Rive, cofounded *SolarCity* back in 2006 with his brother. The two have an astounding commitment to providing the world with clean energy. He remained as the CTO throughout the time that *SolarCity* was run independently. After the takeover by Tesla, Peter Rive went on to stay with the company for eight months before leaving for good.

Soon after, the two brothers, Peter and Lyndon, went back to their South African roots and joined a startup. The company, called *Zola Electric*, is focused on providing clean energy to South Africa. The vision of the two brothers remains as they work on creating solutions that will aid in the development of clean energy. One of the main drivers of creating clean energy is solar energy.

The two brothers shifted back in February of 2019 and have continued to set their mark in the startup. They're actively working to bring about a change and create energy-efficient solutions for South Africa. Talk about massive achievements and for a great cause.

Russ Rive

Another cousin from Musk's childhood is Russ Rive. He is the brother of Lyndon and Peter, and they have gone on to have some great memories growing up. Musk's mother would be mainly responsible for the children, leading to them being closer than ever as they grew up.

Russ Rive has also had his fair share of entrepreneurial development, just like his other siblings. In fact, the three of them started the project *Everdream* together before selling it off to *Dell*. While they worked on *Everdream*, Russ went on to work as a CTO for their startup. He is known to be extremely committed to his work as he went on to cofound another organization as well.

He shifted gears once *Everdream* was acquired by *Dell* and went on to explore the world of creative technology. Ever since he has worked on multiple projects and even cofounded a company called *SuperUber*. His designing skills had excelled throughout this time as his work has been exhibited around the world.

More than that, Tesla and SpaceX are proud clients of the production company, *SuperUber*, as well. He was also a part of the initial team when Elon Musk and Kimbal Musk worked on *Zip2*.

Almeda Rive

Lastly, on the cousins' list, we have Almeda Rive. She is the sister of Russ, Peter, and Lyndon Rive and a proud cousin of Elon. While almost every cousin and sibling of Musk proved to have some entrepreneurial linkage, Almeda made sure to go a completely different way when it came to her career choice. You will find her choice to be more unique than her siblings, as it is something that you would not expect.

Born in 1986, the youngest of them all, Almeda went on to become a competitive dirt bike rider. Who would have thought? Now, you know that the Musk family is a mixture of completely different people. Each of them has their own aspirations as they follow what they want to. There's nothing holding them back.

There is not much more detail about Almeda Rive other than that she might have worked in the sales department of SolarCity at some point. But there aren't any clear identifications as to what role she played while working in the company.

Elon Musk's Wives

We are all done with the siblings and cousins. It is now time to move on to Elon Musk's wives. He has been married twice. Well, if you count his marriage to his second wife twice, there is a total of three marriages. Let's take a closer look at his marriages now.

Justine Musk

Musk's first wife, Justine Wilson, born in 1972, is a renowned Canadian author. The two met while they were studying at the same university, Queen's University in Ontario. While there wasn't anything going on at this time, the two were parted as Musk went on to join the University of Pennsylvania.

Justine and Musk reconnected after they were done with their graduation. At that time, Musk was establishing his very first startup, and Justine was working on her novel. The two of them tied the knot in 2000 and lived a married life for about eight years. The couple shifted to Los Angeles to spend their lives together there.

Musk and Justine had six children from their marriage, out of which one died within ten weeks after birth. There were triplets and twins that Justine gave birth to. All their children were born using IVF (In Vitro Fertilization).

While the two stayed together for about eight years, they called it quits in 2008. Justine has gone on to say that their marriage was not the best; it was actually unhealthy for both of them. After calling it quits, Justine went on to continue her writing. The two of them remain on decent terms.

Talulah Riley

Next, we have Musk's second wife, Talulah Riley, the British actress. The two might have had something going on while Musk was married because they got engaged within six weeks of his divorce with Justine. This leaves many questioning his loyalty to his first wife.

Musk and Talulah remained engaged for the next two years, and then finally tied the knot in 2010. But soon after, during 2012, there was news that the two were splitting up. A tweet by Musk confirmed it all when he said, "It was an amazing four years. I will love you forever. You will make someone very happy one day."

Now, you might think that this was over, but it wasn't. The two remarried in 2013 and went on to live a year longer of a successful marriage before Musk filed for divorce again in 2014. This was withdrawn, and the two remained together till 2016. This was when they called it quits for good. Riley filed for divorce this time, and it was finalized before the year ended.

While it may seem like they had a troubled relationship because of the two divorces, it turned out great.

The two of them are in great places right now, and they're always rooting for each other. The divorce didn't seem to put them in a bad place. They're on good terms and meet up with each other from time to time. The two did not have any children while they were together.

Children of Elon Musk

When it comes to Musk's children, he had six children from his first wife, no children from his second wife, and only one child from his girlfriend, Grimes. Five of his children from his first wife are still alive and are bound to have great guidance from the entrepreneurial family that they have been born into. With their father a mastermind in the tech industry, there is surely a lot expected from the young ones.

While they are still very young at this point, there is a lot for them to learn as they grow alongside their father. So, finally, let's take a look at Elon Musk's children.

Nevada Alexander Musk

Nevada Alexander musk was born in 2002 to Elon and Justine Musk. While they rejoiced in the birth of their son, little did they know that he would leave them very quickly. The infant passed away when he was only ten weeks old.

The reason for the death was SIDS (Sudden Infant Death Syndrome), which left the family at a loss for a long time. Moving forward, they made use of different methods to have children in the future.

The Twins: Griffin and Xavier Musk

After a couple of years, Justine and Elon tried for children again. This time, they made sure to make use of methods that would lessen any complications. They opted for IVF (In Vitro Fertilization) for their children. This proved to be highly effective as their twins came into this world, Griffin and Xavier Musk. The two were born in 2004 in Pretoria and remain healthy to date. Their father is like a role model to them, and they enjoy each other's company.

The Triplets: Kai, Damian, and Saxon Musk

A couple of years later, Justine and Elon tried for children again. And, again, they went for the IVF option. This led to them having triplets, namely, Kai, Damian, and Saxon Musk. The three boys became a great addition to the family of four. Now, the family stood at seven members, with five boys that brought a lot of energy into their home. These three were born in 2006, putting a two-year difference between the twins and themselves. But it wasn't long before the family was broken apart. Justine was out of the picture after a couple of years of the triplets' birth because of some unresolvable issues with Musk. While she continued to carry out her motherly duties, the children mainly stayed with their father. This allowed Musk to create a stronger bond with his sons.

Elon Musk's Youngest Child's Name is X Æ A-12

These days, people look for unique names for their kids. However, no one can beat the creativity of mastermind Elon Musk in naming his child. "X Æ A-12." That's the name Musk and singer Grimes gave to their newborn baby—a mere sequence of some letters of the alphabet, a special symbol, and a number. When they declared this name after the delivery of a healthy boy, people considered it a trick or brain-twister, leading to the real name. A lot of theories popped up on the internet to guess the meaning of this name before it was explained by the couple. One such speculation made the name's pronunciation as "Kyle." The logic behind it included the "K" sound of X, which is the Greek letter Chi, the "ai" sound of the symbol Æ, and the letter "L" representing A-12 in the alphabetical series. However, Musk has cleared away all clouds of mystery about how it would correctly be pronounced. The symbol in the middle is verbalized as "ash," making the name emerge as "X-Ash-A-12."

Let's take a look at what Musk and Grimes have to say about this unique name. Musk explained it very well in an interview with Joe Rogan, who was hosting a podcast show. Grimes also elaborated on the significance of the name on Twitter, saying that "X" in the name is the unknown variable. "Æ" denotes her elven spelling, which stands for artificial intelligence and/or love. "A-12" refers to Archangel-12 aircraft. One must know that the Lockheed Archangel-12 is a forerunner to their favorite plane, the SR-71 aircraft. Though this plane represents neither weapons nor defense, it works powerfully in wars without any violence. The couple included it in the baby's name because it has evolved as a classic expression of speed. Moreover, "A" stands for Archangel, which is Grime's beloved song. She played the major role in finding the name as unique as this except for A-12, which was contributed by Musk.

This is certainly an outstanding example of Musk's ability to think beyond boundaries. However, no one can deny the fact that many big shots on the billionaires' list have been caught in conflict with the governing rules because of their "break the rules" concept. Elon Musk is no exception. It must be mentioned that the baby's name is not yet accepted by the California government because the state allows for only 26 English letters and a few more special characters, like apostrophes, hyphens, and periods. It permits no symbols like Æ. Later, it was announced that the parents are changing a little part of the baby's name from A-12 to A-Xii. This change was made not because of Californian laws but because Grimes was inspired by the Roman number XII as a replacement for 12. The question of the symbol in the name remains the same, as the name is now X Æ A-Xii. It is worth waiting to see what Musk does next about it.

SECTION 3
ANALYZING ELON MUSK

CHAPTER ONE

MOST POPULAR QUOTES BY ELON MUSK

"When I was in college, I just thought, 'Well, what are the things that are most likely to affect the future of humanity at a macro level?' And it just seemed like there would be the Internet, sustainable energy, making life multi-planetary, and then genetics and AI."

"We're running the most dangerous experiment in history right now, which is to see how much carbon dioxide the atmosphere [...] can handle before there is an environmental catastrophe."

"I would like to die on Mars. Just not on impact."

"If you go back a few hundred years, what we take for granted today would seem like magic – being able to talk to people over long distances, to transmit images, flying, accessing vast amounts of data like an oracle. These are all things that would have been considered magic a few hundred years ago."

"There have only been about a half dozen genuinely important events in the four-billion-year saga of life on Earth: single-celled life, multi-celled life, differentiation into plants and animals, movement of animals from water to land, and the advent of mammals and consciousness."

"Whenever I'd read about cool technology, it'd tend to be in the United States or, more broadly, North America. [...] I kind of wanted to be where the cutting edge of technology was, and of course within the United States, Silicon Valley is where the heart of things is. Although, at the time, I didn't know where Silicon Valley was. It sounded like some mythical place."

"If anyone thinks they'd rather be in a different part of history, they're probably not a very good student of history. Life sucked in the old days. People knew very little, and you were likely to die at a young age of some horrible disease. You'd probably have no teeth by now. It would be particularly awful if you were a woman."

"We're already a cyborg. You have a digital version of yourself or partial version of yourself online in the form of your e-mails and your social media and all the things that you do. And you have, basically, superpowers with your computer and your phone and the applications that are there. You have more power than the president of the United States had 20 years ago. You can answer any question; you can video conference with anyone anywhere; you can send a message to millions of people instantly. You just do incredible things."

"The fundamental problem with cities is that we build cities in 3D. You've got these tall buildings with lots of people on each floor, but then you've got roads, which are 2D. That obviously just doesn't work. You're guaranteed to have gridlock. But you can go 3D if you have tunnels. And you can have many tunnels crisscrossing each other with maybe a few meters of vertical distance between them and completely get rid of traffic problems."

"It wasn't like, 'Oh, I want to make a bunch of money.' [...] With the Internet, anyone who had a connection anywhere in the world would have access to all the world's information, just like a nervous system. Humanity was effectively becoming a super organism and qualitatively different than what it had been before, and so I wanted to be part of that."

"Going from PayPal, I thought: 'Well, what are some of the other problems that are likely to most affect the future of humanity?' Not from the perspective, 'What's the best way to make money?'"

"I think the profit motive is a good one if the rules of an industry are properly set up. There is nothing fundamentally wrong with profit. In fact, profit just means that people are paying you more for whatever you're doing that you're spending to create it. That's a good thing."

"The reality is gas prices should be much more expensive than they are because we're not incorporating the true damage to the environment and the hidden costs of mining oil and transporting it to the U.S. Whenever you have an unpriced externality, you have a bit of a market failure, to the degree that externality remains unpriced."

"[The Hitchhikers Guide to the Galaxy] taught me that the tough thing is figuring out what questions to ask, but that once you do that, the rest is really easy. I came to the conclusion that we should aspire to increase the scope and scale of human consciousness in order to better understand what questions to ask. Really, the only thing that makes sense is to strive for greater collective enlightenment."

"A lot of kids are in school puzzled as to why they're there. I think if you can explain the 'why' of things, then that makes a huge difference to people's motivation. Then they understand purpose."

"It shouldn't be that you've got these grades where people move in lockstep and everyone goes through English, math, science, and so forth from fifth grade to sixth grade to seventh grade like it's an assembly line. People are not objects on an assembly line. That's a ridiculous notion. People learn and are interested in different things at different paces. You really want to disconnect the whole grade-level thing from the subjects. Allow people to progress at the fastest pace that they can or are interested in, in each subject. It seems like a really obvious thing."

"I never had a job where I made anything physical. I cofounded two Internet software companies, Zip2 and PayPal. So it took me a few years to kind of learn rocket science, if you will.

I had to learn how you make hardware. I'd never seen a CNC machine or laid out carbon fibre. I didn't know any of these things. But if you read books and talk to experts, you'll pick it up pretty quickly. [...] It's really pretty straightforward. Just read books and talk to people—particularly books. The data rate of reading is much greater than when somebody's talking. You can learn whatever you need to do to start a successful business either in school or out of school. A school, in theory, should help accelerate that process, and I think oftentimes it does. It can be an efficient learning process, perhaps more efficient than empirically learning lessons. There are examples of successful entrepreneurs who never graduated high school, and there are those that have PhDs. I think the important principle is to be dedicated to learning what you need to know, whether that is in school or empirically."

"I do think a good framework for thinking is physics, you know, the first principles reasoning. What I mean by that is boil things down to their fundamental truths and reason up from there as opposed to reasoning by analogy. Through most of our life, we get through life by reasoning by analogy, which essentially means kind of copying what other people do with slight variations. And you have to do that, otherwise mentally you wouldn't be able to get through the day. But when you want to do something new, you have to apply the physics approach. Physics has really figured out how to discover new things that are counterintuitive, like quantum mechanics; it's really counterintuitive."

"I do kinda feel like my head is full! My context-switching penalty is high, and my process isolation is not what it used to be. Frankly, though, I think most people can learn a lot more than they think they can. They sell themselves short without trying. One bit of advice: it is important to view knowledge as sort of a semantic tree—make sure you understand the fundamental principles, i.e., the trunk and big branches, before you get into the leaves/details or there is nothing for them to hang on to."

"Do you have the right axioms, are they relevant, and are you making the right conclusions based on those axioms? That's the essence of critical thinking, and yet it is amazing how often people fail to do that. I think wishful thinking is innate in the human brain. You want things to be the way you wish them to be, and so you tend to filter information that you shouldn't filter."

"When Henry Ford made cheap, reliable cars people said, 'Nah, what's wrong with a horse?' That was a huge bet he made, and it worked."

"It's better to approach this [building a company] from the standpoint of saying—rather than you want to be an entrepreneur or you want to make money—what are some useful things that you do that you wish existed in the world?"

"What a lot of people don't appreciate is that technology does not automatically improve. It only improves if a lot of really strong engineering talent is applied to the problem. [...] There are many examples in history where civilizations have reached a certain technology level and that have fallen well below that and then recovered only millennia later."

"I care a lot about the truth of things and trying to understand the truth of things. I think that's important. If you're going to come up with some solution, then the truth is really, really important."

"Fundamentally, if you don't have a compelling product at a compelling price, you don't have a great company."

"I do think it's worth thinking about whether what you're doing is going to result in disruptive change or not. If it's just incremental, it's unlikely to be something major. It's got to be something that's substantially better than what's gone on before."

"I don't create companies for the sake of creating companies, but to get things done."

"The path to the CEO's office should not be through the CFO's office, and it should not be through the marketing department. It needs to be through engineering and design."

"I want to accentuate the philosophy that I have with companies in the startup phase, which is a sort of 'special forces' approach. The minimum passing grade is excellent. That's the way I believe startup companies need to be if they're ultimately going to be large and successful companies. We'd adhered to that to some degree, but we'd strayed from that path in a few places. That doesn't mean the people that we let go on that basis would be considered bad—it's just the difference between Special Forces and regular Army. If you're going to get through a really tough environment and ultimately grow the company to something significant, you have to have a very high level of dedication and talent throughout the organization."

"I don't think everything needs to change the world; you know. [...] Just say: 'Is what I'm doing as useful as it could be?' 'Whatever this thing is that you're trying to create, what would be the utility delta compared to the current state of the art times how many people it would affect?' That's why I think having something that makes a big difference but affects a small to moderate number of people is great, as is something that makes even a small difference but affects a vast number of people."

"It's important to create an environment that fosters innovation, but you want to let it evolve in a Darwinian way. You don't want to, at a high level, at a gut level, pick a technology and decide that that's the thing that's going to win because it may not be. You should really let things evolve."

"We don't think too much about what competitors are doing because I think it's important to be focused on making the best possible products. It's maybe analogous to what they say about if you're in a race: don't worry about what the other runners are doing—just run."

"I always invest my own money in the companies that I create. I don't believe in the whole thing of just using other people's money. I don't think that's right. I'm not going to ask other people to invest in something if I'm not prepared to do so myself."

"The biggest mistake in general that I've made—and I'm trying to correct for that—is to put too much of a weighting on somebody's talent and not enough on their personality [...]. It actually matters whether somebody has a good heart. It really does. And I've made the mistake of thinking that sometimes it's just about the brain."

"I'm head engineer and chief designer as well as CEO [at SpaceX], so I don't have to cave to some money guy. I encounter CEOs who don't know the details of their technology and that's ridiculous to me."

"We have essentially no patents in SpaceX. Our primary long-term competition is in China. If we published patents, it would be farcical, because the Chinese would just use them as a recipe book."

"Some people don't like change, but you need to embrace change if the alternative is disaster."

"I think it's very important to have a feedback loop, where you're constantly thinking about what you've done and how you could be doing it better."

"Always solicit critical feedback, particularly from friends. Because, generally, they will be thinking it, but they won't tell you."

"If something is important enough, even if the odds are against you, you should still do it."

"The first step is to establish that something is possible; then probability will occur."

"Any product that needs a manual to work is broken."

"Failure is an option here. If things are not failing, you are not innovating enough."

"You're not going to create revolutionary cars or rockets on 40 hours a week. It just won't work. Colonizing Mars isn't going to happen on 40 hours a week."

"Work like hell. I mean you just have to put in 80 to 100-hour weeks every week. [This] improves the odds of success. If other people are putting in 40-hour workweeks and you're putting in 100-hour workweeks, then even if you're doing the same thing, you know that you will achieve in four months what it takes them a year to achieve.

"There's no map. By its nature, it's unknown, which means you're going to make false moves. It must be OK to make false moves."

"A small group of very technically strong people will always beat a large group of moderately strong people."

"Brand is just a perception, and perception will match reality over time. Sometimes it will be ahead, other times it will be behind. But brand is simply a collective impression some have about a product."

"I certainly have lost many battles. So far, I have not lost a war, but I've certainly lost many battles [...] more than I can count, probably.

We came very close to both companies not succeeding in 2008. We had three failures of the SpaceX rocket, so we were 0 for 3. We had the crazy financial recession, the Great Recession. The Tesla financing round was falling apart because it's pretty hard to raise money for a startup car company if GM and Chrysler are going bankrupt. [...] Fortunately, at the end of 2008, the fourth launch, which was the last launch we had money for, worked for SpaceX, and we loved the Tesla financing round Christmas Eve 2008, the last hour of the last day that it was possible."

"From an evolutionary standpoint, human consciousness has not been around very long. A little light just went on after four and a half billion years. How often does that happen? Maybe it is quite rare."

"I think AI is going to be incredibly sophisticated in 20 years. It seems to be accelerating. The tricky thing about predicting things when there is an exponential is that an exponential looks linear close-up. But actually, it's not linear. And AI appears to be accelerating, as far as I can see."

"It's not as though I think the risk is that the AI would develop all on its own right off the bat. The concern is that someone may use it in a way that is bad, and even if they weren't going to use it in a way that is bad, somebody would take it from them and use it in a way that's bad. That, I think, is quite a big danger. We must have democratization of AI technology and make it widely available. That's the reason [we] created OpenAI.

There's a quote that I love from Lord Acton—he was the guy who came up with, 'Power corrupts and absolute power corrupts absolutely'—which is that 'freedom consists of the distribution of power and despotism in its concretion.' I think it's important if we have this incredibly powerful AI that it not be concentrated in the hands of the few."

"Creating a neural lace is the thing that really matters for humanity to achieve symbiosis with machines."

"Hope we're not just the biological boot loader for digital superintelligence. Unfortunately, that is increasingly probable."

If there was a way that I could not eat, so I could work more, I would not eat. I wish there was a way to get nutrients without sitting down for a meal."

"I wouldn't say I have a lack of fear. In fact, I'd like my fear emotion to be less because it's very distracting and fries my nervous system."

"I always have optimism, but I'm realistic. It was not with the expectation of great success that I started Tesla or SpaceX. [...] It's just that I thought they were important enough to do anyway."

"The reality is that autonomous systems will drive orders of magnitude better than people. In terms of accidents per mile, it'll be far lower. Technologically, I think it's about three years away for full autonomy."

"Owning a car that is not self-driving, in the long term, will be like owning a horse—you would own it and use it for sentimental reasons but not for daily use."

"You can only go there every two years because the orbital synchronization of Earth and Mars is about every two years. But I think it would be an interesting way for the civilization to develop. People would meet each other and be like, 'What orbital synchronization did you arrive on?'"

"You need to live in a dome initially, but over time you could terraform Mars to look like Earth and eventually walk around outside without anything on. […] So, it's a fixer-upper of a planet."

"Somewhere along the way Hydrogen started talking and thought it was conscious. The hydrogen became sentient it gradually got more complex."

"As much as possible, avoid hiring MBAs. MBA programs don't teach people how to create companies."

"People work better when they know what the goal is and why. It is important that people look forward to coming to work in the morning and enjoy working."

"There's a tremendous bias against taking risks. Everyone is trying to optimize their ass-covering."

"Starting and growing a business is as much about the innovation, drive, and determination of the people behind it as the product they sell."

"I think we have a duty to maintain the light of consciousness to make sure it continues into the future."

"(Physics is) a good framework for thinking. … Boil things down to their fundamental truths and reason up from there."

"You want to be extra rigorous about making the best possible thing you can. Find everything that's wrong with it and fix it. Seek negative feedback, particularly from friends."

"Persistence is very important. You should not give up unless you are forced to give up."

"You want to have a future where you're expecting things to be better, not one where you're expecting things to be worse."

"Life is too short for long-term grudges."

"You shouldn't do things differently just because they're different. They need to be... better."

"I think life on Earth must be about more than just solving problems... It's got to be something inspiring, even if it is vicarious."

"Why do you want to live? What's the point? What inspires you? What do you love about the future? And if the future's not including being out there among the stars and being a multi-planet species, it's incredibly depressing if that's not the future we're going to have."

"It is a mistake to hire huge numbers of people to get a complicated job done. Numbers will never compensate for talent in getting the right answer (two people who don't know something are no better than one), will tend to slow down progress, and will make the task incredibly expensive."

"A company is a group organized to create a product or service, and it is only as good as its people and how excited they are about creating. I do want to recognize a ton of super-talented people. I just happen to be the face of the companies."

"I do think there is a lot of potential if you have a compelling product and people are willing to pay a premium for that. I think that is what Apple has shown. You can buy a much cheaper cell phone or laptop, but Apple's product is so much better than the alternative, and people are willing to pay that premium."

CHAPTER TWO

ELON MUSK'S OUTSTANDING CHARACTERISTICS AND HABITS

Elon Musk's achievements are inspiring for people all over the world. It doesn't matter what trait you're involved with or what your position is at the moment; Elon Musk's success definitely inspires everyone to rise up and find the same strength that moves him.

When we think about successful people in our time, the likes of Elon Musk, Steve Jobs, Jeff Bezos, etc., there's something they all have in common: an almost maniacal obsession with improvement, blind devotion to their ideas, and an unbreakable sense of commitment to what they believe.

Their characteristics and habits are something we can all learn from and apply to our own lives. These are the traits that have made these men so successful and the world a better place as a consequence.

Imagine what would happen if we would all study these characteristics and habits and applied them to our lives. We wouldn't only learn to be more self-confident, relentless, strong-minded, and willful; we would also improve not only our lives but our surroundings and the lives of the people around us.

That's why today, I want to take a look at some of the most essential characteristics and habits that have helped Elon Musk become the man he is today.

1. INTJ Entrepreneurship

Elon Musk is not an ordinary entrepreneur; he is an INTJ (Introversion, Intuition, Thinking, Judgment) entrepreneur, as his personality dictates. He's an unemotional person when it comes to business, and he looks past what's visible. This is a characteristic that has definitely allowed him to find clear ways to improve his surroundings and look for future improvement.

INTJ entrepreneurs are usually workaholics, which is definitely the case with Elon Musk, and they tend to focus on a single thing at a time with incredible depth of both perception and focus. This means multitasking is out of the question, contrary to popular belief. Another common trait of INTJ entrepreneurs is how relentless they are about their goals, which is something Elon Musk has proven time and time again. No matter what the obstacle or challenge is, they never give up, and that's something we can all benefit from.

2. The Drive to Reach Goals

I want to touch on this subject in a more in-depth manner because this is one of the main characteristics that has made Elon Musk so successful. His motivation and drive to do the things he sets out to do are unparalleled. Anyone of us has buckled under doubt, fear of failure, or obstacles at one point or another, and we have nothing to show for it.

What this means is that single-minded determination and the motivation always to move forward, no matter what is the best way to go about business and about life in general. Never give up; never surrender your desires and dreams in the face of adversity. On the contrary, push forward, make your way, and believe in your ideas. No one else will! Elon Musk met resistance with projects such as Tesla Motors and SpaceX, to name a couple; what did he do? How much did his resilience improve our society? You can do the same.

3. Insane Work Ethics

If you look up the term "workaholic" in the dictionary, it's likely that you'll see a picture of Elon Musk. He's a hardcore workaholic, which means he practices insane work ethics. It's clear to him that there's no shortcut to success; it takes hard work for many years and a lot of dedication to your craft. He makes it his task to be the hardest working employee in the company, and he sets the highest standard for everyone working under his wing.

Elon Musk works 100 hours every week, and this has been his habit for years. His lunch breaks are not even 30 minutes long, and even then, he combines his meal with meetings and emails so he can be even more productive. There's nothing Elon Musk does half-way, and it's definitely not in him to be mediocre. Work is oxygen for him, and he constantly pushes his own limits. This is the kind of attitude that will make anyone who practices it closer to success in their field.

4. Focus on the Bigger Picture

If you look at the work Elon Musk has done so far, and you analyze his main areas of focus, which are space, clean energy, and the Internet, you'll notice that he's targeting some of the most challenging areas. That's because Elon Musk's big picture is all about making the world a better place. This means he's willing and ready to take significant risks for his visions for the future.

The ability to keep an eye on the bigger picture and the future of his ideas is what allows him to move toward them with so much efficiency. He believes in what he's doing, and that's why he defends his ideas from anyone who doesn't believe in what he's doing. If there's one thing we need to learn from Elon Musk is his extraordinary goal-setting skills and how he pours his mind, heart, and soul into anything he does.

5. Unconventional Work Methods

Elon Musk has revolutionized every industry he gets his hands on. The most excellent example of his unconventional work methods is Tesla Motors. With the birth of this company, the automotive industry changed forever. Before that, the business model remained unchanged, but Elon Musk saw the opportunity to improve the standard, to raise it, and to offer an unconventional, futuristic product.

The same thing happened when he entered the space and aeronautics industry. His SpaceX company faced the likes of giants like Boeing, but he didn't shy away from the challenge. The idea of reusable rockets revolutionized the industry, and the cost-cutting strategies he has introduced are unparalleled. His unconventional work methods and his desire to break the standard and improve it is one of the many keys to his success. This is something we can all learn to apply to any aspect of our lives, but especially in business.

6. Strong Belief in Self-Analysis

Another outstanding characteristic about Elon Musk is that he doesn't shy away from self-analysis, and he directs his critical thinking to himself as much as he does to everything else. This is difficult to accomplish because we often protect ourselves from ourselves, but it is indeed possible to look at yourself objectively so you can determine what you can do to be better every day.

The key to practicing self-analysis is being honest with yourself and critical about what you're doing. There are things we all believe about ourselves, but it's definitely a mistake to take them for granted. What we need to do is analyze ourselves thoroughly and honestly so we can build up the things that must improve. Our biggest obstacle is often ourselves, so being critical and analyzing yourself will allow you to put everything in place.

7. The Ability to Take Risks

Something that makes Elon Musk outstanding is the fact that he goes to great trouble to make his work possible and his goals a reality. He has taken huge risks more than once, to great rewards. He believes in himself and his goals so much that taking significant risks has never been an issue. He's the king of unusual financial moves, and he embodies both the prosperity and impoverishment of his industries.

There's nothing Elon Musk hasn't done to support and help his ventures, from personal loans to buying stocks. When he invests, he invests everything he has in projects he believes in, even when there's a significant risk of bankruptcy. A great example of this is what happened at the end of 2008 when both Tesla and SpaceX were going under at the same time. The safest option was choosing between one of the companies and letting the other one go bankrupt. But Elon Musk decided to take all the money he had, split it, and invest it in both companies. The risk was incredible, and he almost went through a nervous breakdown, but he saved both companies.

In other words, if you don't take risks and you shy away from tough decisions, you will compromise your vision and lose more than you'd want. "Be bold and mighty forces will come to your aid.", a motto by which to live.

8. Unconditional Love for His Brand

If you don't love what you've built, who else is going to do it? This is yet another thing we can learn from Elon Musk. His unconditional love for his brand and his companies is evidenced not just in his business moves and projects but also in the way he talks about his industry. His work is personal to him, and it's something he holds dear; it's not an obligation. He birthed his companies, nurtures them, and guards them fiercely.

Elon Musk has a strong belief that to be successful at leading others; you need to teach them how to love your brand as much as you do and to treat it accordingly. This should be taught by example, which means your love for the company has to be honest so you can inspire others to dedicate themselves as much as you do. This will earn you fierce allies and colleagues, which will, in turn, make your work a bit easier.

9. Celebration of Success

Even though Elon Musk works a whopping 20 hours a day, he always makes time to enjoy life and his own accomplishments. When you're the head of a company or any group of people who are working towards a common goal, it is vital to take the time to celebrate your success with the people you work with. Expressing gratitude is essential when you work with others, and Elon Musk understands that.

In Musk's own words: if there's something Tesla is good at is throwing parties, and this is evident in the fact that he threw an unbelievable soccer stadium party in 2016. Imagine that! It's safe to say he takes his gratitude for employees seriously. What's more, he enjoys the fruits of his labor by treating himself to things such as an 1800 square-foot condo and a million-dollar McLaren F1 car, to name a few.

10. "Never Stop Learning" Attitude

Last but not least, let's talk about Elon Musk's "never stop learning" attitude. There's nothing Elon Musk is doing that he doesn't strive to understand. He studies his industry; he eats information, and, for him, it's never too late to understand anything, no matter how complex the subject may be.

For one, he's self-taught in programming and many advanced subjects, he reads about a great variety of topics, and he treats knowledge with reverence. Of course, dedicating yourself to learning as much as you can about the things that interest you will take time, and it also requires a method.

For Elon Musk, that method consists of viewing knowledge as a semantic tree. What he does is understand the fundamental principles of the subject first, which represent the trunk and the big branches of the tree, before he moves on to the leaves, which are the details. This is a great method, and it has allowed him to master many different subjects in a short amount of time. Being efficient about the way you learn is essential if you want to move forward and move faster.

Overall, there's quite a lot to learn from Elon Musk's characteristics, habits, and the way he approaches both his life and his work. He's not one of the most successful men in history for nothing! We're lucky enough to have a window into his methods so we can learn as much as we can from the example he sets.

Success doesn't come freely, and it takes a lot of work. The key to success is becoming a successful person, and that's only possible if we dedicate ourselves to developing the skills we need.

CHAPTER THREE

ACHIEVEMENTS AND GOALS OF ELON MUSK

Introduction

Few men of our age are quite as celebrated, achieved, and ambitious as Elon Musk.

The genius engineer-entrepreneur, industrial designer, and philanthropist is known just as much for his eccentric goals as he is for his long list of achievements. With several seemingly impossible achievements already under his belt, the Tesla and SpaceX founder looks to tackle a new list of hard-to-accomplish goals that range from revolutionizing transportation to colonizing Mars.

In this chapter, I will list and detail all of Musk's achievements and goals so you can get a better idea of who he really is, the role he's playing in the world, and the impact he could have on the future.

Let's start!

Achievements

To begin with, let's detail all the incredible feats Elon Musk has already achieved, starting with his early years. With achievements ranging from "small" feats such as adolescent video game programming to world-changing events such as creating the world's best-selling line of electric cars, Musk has quite the full resume.

- **1984—Created Blastar**

    At the age of twelve, most children are happy simply playing video games. They certainly aren't researching the game mechanics and writing source code. But that's exactly what Elon Musk did in 1984.

At just twelve years of age, he wrote the code for a game he called "Blastar." The game's mission? To destroy alien space freighters carrying potentially deadly nuclear material.

In the game, players are given five lives (or spaceships) to defeat oncoming enemies. Though there are never more than two enemies on screen at the same time, players must be careful to avoid their deadly "status beams," which can be fired from enemy vessels and take out one of the player's lives.

Though the game was largely a simple one compared to Space Invaders and some others at the time, the accomplishment is worthwhile considering Musk's age at the time of creation. In recent interviews, Musk has called the game "trivial," but has noted that it was still "...better than Flappy Bird."

With a playable version online, you can decide for yourself whether that last statement is true or not. What's clear is that *PC and Office Technology* magazine thought the game was a steal at the time. The publication bought the rights to the game for $500 from the young Musk, marking his first successful foray into capitalism.

• 1994—Graduated from the University of Pennsylvania

In 1994, Musk graduated from the University of Pennsylvania with a double degree in economics from the prestigious Wharton School and physics from the College of Arts and Sciences. This marked Musk's most significant educational achievement and fulfilled his dream of graduating from an American university.

Before going to the university, he had attended Queen's University in Kingston (Canada). He landed in the U.S. as a transfer student to the University of Pennsylvania. Besides marking a significant educational achievement in his life, Musk's time at the University of Pennsylvania also foreshadowed his future as a genius entrepreneur: while there, Musk successfully ran an underground nightclub.

- **1995—Founded Zip2**

Following successful graduation from the University of Pennsylvania, Musk immediately applied for and dropped out of Stanford's PhD program for physics. The reason was simple: the young Elon Musk desired his second crack at capitalism.

In 1999, after helping run the company for four years, Musk participated in the selling of Zip2.

This marked the first time that Musk profited wildly from his ventures, and it gave him the necessary capital to fund his next achievement: X.com.

- **1999—Helped Form X.com and PayPal**

When X.com and PayPal were sold to eBay in 2001, Musk received quite the pretty penny.

Through Zip2 and PayPal, Musk had earned millions of dollars before the age of 30. Interestingly, however, this would look minor compared to the serial entrepreneur's next achievements.

- **2002—Founded SpaceX**

The company started with one goal: to help grow the space industry and find pathways to Mars colonization that could secure the future of mankind by making humans an interplanetary species.

That's a pretty broad goal, but SpaceX has blazed through its own list of achievements.

In 2008, NASA awarded SpaceX a contract of over $1 billion for Commercial Resupply Services (CRS) to the International Space

Station. In 2009, Falcon 9 rocket by SpaceX fulfilled this contract and made history.

In 2010, SpaceX became the first private company to launch a new version of Falcon 9 into orbit and recovered a spacecraft successfully. This proved the success of their rocket technology.

By the end of 2010, SpaceX's Dragon cargo capsule was the first privately developed spacecraft in history that could launch and re-enter from low-Earth orbit.

By the end of 2013, a Falcon 9 rocket successfully launched to Geosynchronous Transfer Orbit (GTO) for the very first time in history.

In 2014, SpaceX successfully soft-landed a Falcon 9 rocket's first stage in the Atlantic Ocean.

In 2015, the Falcon 9 delivered 11 communications satellites in orbit. It successfully returned from space and landed at Landing Zone 1, becoming the first orbital-class rocket in history to land on the pad.

In 2018, SpaceX successfully launched a Tesla Roadster with Starman on the debut flight of Falcon Heavy. Both these rocket boosters landed simultaneously.

In 2019, SpaceX conducted the maiden launch of Crew Dragon.

- **2004—Became Chairman of Tesla**

As chairman, Musk helped oversee the direction of the first-ever Tesla vehicle: the industry-redefining Roadster. Though the Roadster would not be released for four more years, Musk, along with CEO Martin Eberhard and CFO Marc Tarpenning, played a defining role in the development of the vehicle.

In the time before becoming CEO of Tesla, Musk largely oversaw operations—though not on a day-to-day basis. Instead, former Tesla

Motors employees recall Musk popping in from time to time to demand changes on certain aspects of the Roadster.

This input would eventually lead the Roadster to enormous success. Still, it wasn't until later, when Musk took the expanded role as CEO, that Tesla transformed into the giant we recognize today. The steps that led up to Musk's achievement of the CEO position were rocky and involved a number of influencing factors.

- **2008—Became CEO of Tesla**

Becoming CEO of Tesla was certainly a transformational moment in the life of Elon Musk. However, it wasn't always clear that the engineer-entrepreneur would land the position. In fact, tensions between Musk and founder and original CEO Martin Eberhard appeared to cast down on Musk's relationship with the company.

In the months leading up to Eberhard's ousting, the two men engaged in bitter email conflicts about the direction of the company. With the hit of the 2008 recession, especially, Eberhard was viewed as unable to move the company in the right direction. For this reason—and for Eberhard's significant disagreements with Musk and others on Musk's side of the debate—the original CEO was ousted from the firm in 2008. Eberhard's vacancy left an open position, for which Musk was prime for the taking.

Musk, who had already served as CEO of X.com and who was heavily involved in Tesla planning and development operations, saw the vacancy as an opportunity to run Tesla the way he saw fit. Fortunately, shareholders agreed. In 2008, just months after Eberhard's ousting, Musk was named the CEO of Tesla—and the company hasn't looked back since.

In the time since Musk earned the Tesla CEO position, the company has unveiled many successful electric vehicles that have come to reshape the electric car industry. For this reason, Tesla ranked as the best-selling plug-in passenger automobile manufacturer in 2018, earning 12% of all plug-in segment sales. Since 2017 alone, Tesla has seen an increase of 280% in its number of car sales, putting it squarely at number one when it comes to the electric car industry.

- **2013—Unveiled the Hyperloop**

In 2013, Musk unveiled one of his most ambitious ideas to date: the Hyperloop.

While the company hasn't yet established its system, it has tested a number of successful prototypes. In 2015-2016, Musk held Hyperloop pod competitions that saw competitors from all across the world compete in making the first Hyperloop prototypes.

Though many of Musk's Hyperloop dreams have yet to be realized, the amount of success the genius has had generating excitement and plans for the revolutionary transportation system can already be considered a success. In discussing the Hyperloop, the genius engineer has popularized the notion of a more functional and reliable transportation system that—theoretically—could get passengers from LA to San Francisco in just thirty minutes.

- **2015—Founded OpenAI**

Elon Musk has long been a skeptic of increasingly intelligent AI systems that the brilliant entrepreneur believes could one day supplant the human race as the most intelligent species. In recent interviews, Musk has stated that humankind is dangerously close to developing powerful AI technology that will be able to keep itself alive. Joining others such as Bill Gates, Musk echoes the need for a human answer to future AI systems.

Enter OpenAI, one of the genius's most daring achievements yet. Started in 2015, the company looks to use the best talent worldwide to develop human-friendly AI systems that can one day counter independent machine intelligence.

Though this may sound like science fiction, Musk has stated that the company is making significant strides. And while there's not much we can know about the specific development of Musk's AI, the genius entrepreneur has been quick to call the startup a success.

This can be seen in the products that the non-profit has released. Among these are Robosumo, a program that allows meta-learning robots to adapt to changing conditions and apply localized intelligence to broader contexts.

The non-profit has also released Debate Game, a 2018 program that teaches machines how to debate problems in front of a human judge. OpenAI's involvement in such projects is allowing humanity to develop AI that is safer and more beneficial to humans.

Companies around the world may soon be able to look to OpenAI programs for higher applications of machine learning.

- **2016—Founded Neuralink**

Not all aspects of Musk's AI development are open to the public, however. In 2016, the genius founded Neuralink, a company that aims to fight the elimination of the human species at the hands of artificial intelligence.

While Musk initially conceived the idea as a way of helping people with disabilities overcome their shortcomings through AI, the company has since grown into a broader project that aims at increasing general human intelligence.

The goal is to make humans "one" with AI through integrated systems that would give mankind access to a wide variety of information in milliseconds.

While we'll have to wait to evaluate Neuralink's products, it's clear that Musk has managed a significant achievement with Neuralink: the ability to affect the future of humankind through powerful AI technology.

- **2016—Founded the Boring Company**

  2016 also saw the founding of Musk's Boring Company, which aims at revolutionizing transportation by reducing the cost of underground tunnel drilling. The company, which plays a broader role in Musk's dreams of more efficient transportation, has already achieved some success.

The above achievements chronicle a lifetime of work for the eccentric genius entrepreneur. In the years to come, we can surely expect this list to grow exponentially. Until then, we must watch closely as Musk tackles each of his major goals.

The following section contains a list of all the serial entrepreneur's goals. Let's take a look and see what may be in store for us in the near future.

Goals

What professional and personal goals does the CEO and product architect of Tesla, Inc. hold? Though some may sound far-fetched to the average man, Elon Musk is no stranger to dreaming big. The cultural icon has some of the loftiest goals we've ever encountered, all of which are listed below.

- **Commercialize Electric Cars**

  Musk's goal of commercializing electric cars has earned him the reputation of being an eco-friendly entrepreneur. And though we've seen how Musk has already worked to revolutionize the electric car industry, the tech genius still has a few lofty goals to achieve.

Currently, Musk's most ambitious goal for the commercialization of electric cars is likely that half of all US vehicles will be electric by 2027. It's a move that would be more than just a huge success for Musk—it's one that would benefit the eco-friendly movement and the world as a whole.

What would that mean for consumers? The biggest boon may be the fact that the elimination of gas-powered cars would help save out-of-pocket costs.

But Musk doesn't stop there. The engineering genius has already started building electric car charging stations all across the nation and hopes to make them commonplace before the commercialization of electric vehicles. These stations would allow drivers to charge their cars as they travel across the country.

Musk doesn't just want to commercialize family vehicles, however. The genius also looks to create a fleet of new electric-powered semi-trucks that would redefine commercial shipping as we know it. By creating commercial electric transportation options, Musk would secure another large win for the eco-friendly movement—and one for the electric car industry itself. With many believing that electric cars were on their deathbed following the failure of GM's electric model, the creation of large, eighteen-wheeled shipping vehicles would serve as one of the most improbable wins of Musk's career.

And that's not all.

Musk has also reimagined the quintessential American pickup truck. These famous gas-guzzlers have long been a staple of American culture—but Musk now looks to bring them into the twenty-first century. His goal of creating and commercializing electric pick-up trucks modernizes the American vision as a whole.

Though some have expressed their belief that Musk's goals of commercialization are still a long way off yet, the genius entrepreneur remains confident that his goals will come true within the next decade. And as anyone familiar with Elon Musk knows, sometimes it's best not to doubt the genius.

With production started on many of these projects, Musk has already taken the first step of turning these goals into a reality. If his visions come true, we may find ourselves living in an eco-friendlier age of electric cars faster than anyone thought possible.

Anyone, that is, except for Elon Musk.

- **Revolutionize Transportation**

Commercializing electric cars proves to be just one way in which Musk has reimagined world transportation.

In fact, when looking at the grand scheme of things, it may be one of his more reasonable goals. The Tesla CEO has made a name for himself for his eco-friendly practices and lofty visions of commercialized electric car transportation.

But it's his other goals of revolutionizing transportation that have perhaps earned him the most time in the spotlight.

For instance, his goal to create and commercialize self-driving cars has become one of the genius entrepreneur's most-talked-about ambitions.

Perhaps that's because some of his cars are already in production, with some models to be released in 2020. This marks a major innovation in the automotive industry, but Musk isn't quite done yet.

The genius predicts that all cars will be fully autonomous by 2027—meaning that they could drive by themselves. These cars would be able to better protect consumers in the case of an emergency and could even prevent accidents in cases of distracted driving—or even when someone falls asleep at the wheel.

With his self-driving cars in production, it may not be hard to see this goal of Musk's coming true. As always, however, he takes this goal to the next level by suggesting that humans won't even need steering wheels on their devices by 2037. This would mark a major turning point in automotive innovation, as it would mean that artificial intelligence systems would reach enough sophistication to match—or even exceed—the abilities of human drivers.

Elon's latest goals include selling motor vehicle insurance for Tesla vehicles and a 'Robotaxi' plan for a self-driving ride-sharing network - the Tesla Network.

But it wouldn't be Elon Musk if the goals didn't get even bigger. Musk now envisions a world in which major destinations can be reached through the use of underground tunnels and electric sleds. These sleds would propel cars to their destination—cutting down on unnecessary traffic and changing the face of human transportation forever.

As of now, Musk notes that these tunnels are too expensive to build. That's why he's developed the Boring Company to reduce the cost of drilling underground tunnels by a factor of ten.

Though Musk hasn't really given a timeline of when he believes this revolutionized transportation will exist, he's working hard to make it a reality.

This desire to revolutionize the transportation industry can also be seen through his ambitious hyperloop. The goal of the project, Musk notes, is to have vehicles hover along tracks at the speed of sound— changing transportation as we know it.

These lofty goals from Elon Musk may seem like something out of a science-fiction novel. But as the Founder, CEO, and Lead Designer of

SpaceX, has proven several times over, he's got a habit of achieving everything he sets his mind to.

Could this mean that we'll be living in a new age of electric transportation within the next decade?

Elon Musk certainly thinks so.

- **Colonize Mars**

When it comes to his bold—or perhaps even "crazy" goals—Musk doesn't back down or attempt to keep them secret. Since the founding of his mega-successful SpaceX in 2002, Musk has publicly stated a need for humankind to colonize Mars.

In fact, you could say that it's one of the engineering genius's biggest goals and one that he's working tirelessly to achieve. In early 2019, Musk test-launched the first SpaceX craft that will eventually head to Mars. But just how quickly does the genius envision mankind on Mars?

Musk plans on reaching Mars via unmanned rockets by 2022. Though the date remains open to speculation, what's sure is this: if the company can get two cargo ships safely to the red planet within the next few years, it will finally be time to send humanity to Mars.

Just how will this work? With a tentative 2024 date, SpaceX plans on sending two crew ships to Mars with the goal of establishing a propellant production plant. Part of a broader attempt by the company to establish relaunch or "hopping" pads, this propellant plant would use carbon dioxide, ice, and Martian water to create the necessary fuel for a return trip to Earth.

But Musk's goals don't just end there. He believes that his SpaceX astronauts will also be able to cultivate agriculture on Mars through the use of solar-powered hydroponics, a technological innovation already used down here on Earth to facilitate plant growth.

Once these steps are complete, the pathway to Mars colonization is burst wide open—and SpaceX will be squarely leading at the front. If the company is able to successfully complete the aforementioned goals, Musk believes that his company will be able to achieve Mars colonization within the next decade.

In fact, that's one of the stated goals of SpaceX. With the groundwork currently being laid, it's possible that, by the end of our lifetimes, Mars colonization is seen as the norm—and no longer as a pipe dream. Perhaps this is why Musk has stated that there's a 70% chance he'll visit Mars himself before he dies.

By colonizing Mars, Musk hopes to secure a pathway to survival for the human species. While only time will tell if the Founder, CEO, and Lead Designer of SpaceX's efforts will be a success, the current state of SpaceX provides hope that we'll be able to witness the first man on Mars before we're all too much older.

- **Commercialize Interplanetary Transport**

But successfully bringing people to the red planet isn't enough for Musk. While the concept of Mars colonization is one the genius thinks could ultimately save humankind, the SpaceX founder also dreams of the commercialization of broader interplanetary space travel. Under this system, Musk hypothesizes, humans will be able to go from planet to planet and truly see what the galaxy is all about.

That's why SpaceX is currently working on the Interplanetary Transport System (ITS). Musk defines the ITS as a future transportation system that will be able to take mankind through space. Of course, the system's first challenge will be its maiden 2022 launch to Mars.

But how exactly will the ITS work? The idea is actually simpler than you may think—at least on the surface. The ITS seeks to use human-rated spacecraft, fully reusable launch vehicles, effective launch mounts, and on-orbit propellant tankers to successfully bring interplanetary rockets from one destination to the other.

While the success of the ITS largely hinges on its upcoming manned mission to Mars (which seeks to bring about a dozen individuals to the red planet in 2024), it's clear that Musk has broad goals in regard to its ability to transport humans across the galaxy. While admitting that the system might be expensive at first, that it might only be a matter of time before humans can effectively move to Mars for the "low" rates of just $500,000 apiece.

Or, as the genius recently corrected himself in an onstage presentation, perhaps even $100,000 apiece.

While that seems like a hefty price tag, there's no denying that potentially affordable Mars colonization could fundamentally alter the human landscape. For this reason, it's safe to call the ITS one of Musk's most daring goals. With SpaceX currently working overtime to make interplanetary travel a reality, we can only wait to see the results. In all actuality, the process of Mars colonization and interplanetary transport could take much longer than Musk envisions.

Still, if anyone can make affordable travel to and from the red planet a "thing," it would be the innovative genius who has already played a revolutionizing role in life on Earth.

- **Increase Human Intelligence through AI**

We've already touched a little on how Musk is using his OpenAI and Neuralink companies to transform human intelligence, but what specific goals does the engineering genius have for these companies in the years to come?

Specifically, Musk wishes to use his AI technology for two reasons: helping those with disabilities and equipping humans for the fight against powerfully-intelligent machines. In regard to goals, the former may be quicker to achieve than the latter.

Still, Musk believes that he can develop fully-integrated AI technology that will give humans access to higher intelligence by 2027. This would potentially work by elevating human intelligence through chips implanted in the brain.

This goal certainly sounds like science fiction to some—if not most—and Musk knows it. In interviews, the genius entrepreneur has touted his familiarity with the subject and cited existential threat as a reason for his focus on AI development.

Most recently, the genius has scheduled a potential 2019 release for his first wave of Neuralink technology. In a 2018 Joe Rogan podcast, Musk stated plans for an upcoming product that will allow consumers to connect their brains to computers and have increased intelligence.

In discussing the product, the genius engineer stated, "Best case scenario, we potentially merge with AI."

That's some pretty strong language, and, if true, means that Musk may be close to fulfilling one of his longtime and potentially farthest-reaching goals.

The genius believes that the technology could make humankind "vastly" smarter. While Neuralink largely operates in secrecy, it appears consumers will soon get a firsthand look at top-of-the-line AI technology that better tells us the direction Elon Musk is taking and how close the genius entrepreneur is to fulfilling his goals.

- **Popularize Solar Energy**

When Musk acquired solar energy powerhouse SolarCity for $2.6 billion in 2016, many questioned his motives. Musk, however, did not let this criticism deter him from his primary goal: to popularize solar energy.

In a statement regarding Tesla's SolarCity acquisition, Musk stated, "The opportunity here is to have a highly innovative sustainable-energy company that answers the whole energy question from power generation and storage to transport."

From this statement alone, the goal is simple: Musk wishes to make his Tesla company completely energy efficient. By developing cars that rely 100% on clean and affordable energy, Musk believes that his company can help combat the climate crisis.

That's why the engineering genius has quickly used SolarCity to produce a line of Tesla solar panels he thinks will bring affordable solar energy to millions across the country. With Tesla's brand strength, this solar power looks to introduce clean energy to a new and expanded market.

All this is part of Musk's dream to move away from unsafe energy sources of the past. A major critic of fossil fuels, Musk is an outspoken advocate for the popularization of renewable energy sources that can help save the Earth from global warming and effectively secure a greater and more stable future for the human race.

The Bottom Line

It's not easy keeping up with Elon Musk.

In fact, it often feels like Elon has a new project every day. For most of us, it can be a rollercoaster ride trying to keep up with one of the world's most innovative minds. Still, it's worth knowing what he is up to and what he plans for the future.

That's why I compiled this list of every achievement Elon Musk has ever made. What's more, I have added all of his goals so that readers can get a better idea of where the genius is headed in the future.

As time passes, it's guaranteed that some of the goals listed here will undoubtedly move to the "achievements" section. Until that time comes, all we can do is watch Musk from afar and add to this list whenever he proposes another revolutionary idea.

When did Elon's Mother Know That He was a Special Child?

We all know the degree of talent that Elon Musk has demonstrated in his life. However, the roots of his talent were spotted by his mother at a very early age. The high IQ society Mensa International has given 17 signs that a child could be a genius, most of which are quite identifiable in Elon Musk. Some of these include an unusual memory and reading early. Musk's mother, Maye Musk, highlights that Musk not only started reading very early but also read everything. When Musk was young, his parents began to live apart. Musk's father had the Encyclopedia Britannica, which his mother could not afford. Hungry to read the encyclopedia, Musk liked to stay with his father. Musk finished reading the entire Encyclopedia Britannica and Collier's Encyclopedia at the age of nine. This was when Maye Musk realized that she was blessed by the birth of a special child. What was uncommon is that he, with his unusual memory, remembered everything he read. That's why he was called a "Genius Boy," as told by his mother. It is worth noting that there was no internet in those days; otherwise, they would have called him the internet, she admits. His potential and determination since his early childhood surprised his mother. From then onwards, he kept exploring his talent in all ways possible.

Curiosity is another characteristic of a genius child and this is what Musk was filled with. He was always on the lookout for new information and knowledge to feed his satiable learning appetite. Often remembered as a bookworm, Musk was supposed to be an introverted guy in his childhood. Being bullied in school by other students made him even more so.

Apart from books, another thing he was interested in was technology, computers, and science fiction. As mentioned by Mensa, having unusual hobbies or interests or in-depth knowledge of certain subjects is a sign of a genius child. Musk had convinced his father to purchase a Commodore VIC-20, which was no less than an age-old computer. However, access to computers was very rare in the 1970s. As per the manual of that device, a common man takes around six months to learn the basics. Musk completed it in just three days, again proving his genius by learning so quickly. Musk's mother was astonished to see a child stay awake for three straight days to complete a hard task in almost no time. Not stopping at this, he further developed a video game on that computer. Setting a high target for oneself is included in the list of signs of a genius kid by Mensa. Musk, with his exceptional entrepreneurial skills, sold the source code of that video game to a computer magazine for $500. Can you guess his age when this happened? He was just 12!

So, Elon Musk has been observed to have most of the typical behaviors of a genius child that are described by Mensa scientifically.

CHAPTER FOUR

THE OTHER SIDE OF ELON MUSK

Introduction

Visionary. Innovator. Iron Man.

There are countless ways to describe Elon Musk. Over the last decade, the engineer-entrepreneur Tesla and SpaceX CEO has emerged as a leader in the second technological revolution and positioned himself as a dominant cultural figure.

In the course of just a few decades, the tech giant has initiated a wide-scale revolution of the transportation industry and opened the door for Martian colonization. Simply put, Musk's work has been nothing short of game-changing.

As a result, Elon has developed quite the following. Online communities are full of Elon Musk fans who follow him with near-religious fervor. Fans take Musk's word as gold and delight in his frequent appearances on Internet streams and at tech events across the globe.

With all this being said, there's one word that fans frequently leave out when discussing the entrepreneur: imperfect. Though it's fashionable to envision Musk as a perfect, do-it-all innovator with the skills and the mindset to take on and revolutionize the world, the truth of the matter is that Musk, like the rest of us, is human.

And with that humanity come a few flaws.

In this guide, I will break down Elon Musk's negative qualities to get a more accurate look at the genius. Specifically, we'll look at a few of his bad traits, bad habits, and a few of his eyebrow-raising past actions. In doing so, we seek to establish not that Musk is unworthy of his praise—quite the opposite actually.

I believe that viewing Musk holistically for who he is—flaws and all—paints an ever-grander picture of the entrepreneur's life. Namely, despite the fact that he is flawed like the rest of us, Musk is able to overcome his shortcomings and achieve continuous, groundbreaking success.

With that being said, let's jump in and take a more personal look at the cultural icon and tech innovator who is rapidly changing the world we live in.

Bad Traits

Let's start by taking a look at some of the negative traits Elon has displayed over the course of his career. The bad traits listed here come from interviews with former Musk employees, those who know him well, and from widely-publicized events that helped shed light on who he truly is behind the scenes.

- **Demanding**

  A look at Musk's past employees and statements made by the entrepreneur himself show one common thread: Musk is demanding. Musk, who regularly pulls 120-hour workweeks, has been known to expect the same from his Tesla and SpaceX employees.

  When one employee complained about long work hours, Musk allegedly had this to say, "I would tell those people that they would get to see their families a lot when we go bankrupt."

  The message? If you don't want to do the work, you can leave. It's clear that Musk doesn't expect any nonsense at his organizations. This demanding nature can cause strife between Musk and his employees, who often feel intimidated by the genius engineer's strict work schedule.

  Musk has also been quoted as saying, "That's my lesson for taking a vacation. Vacation will kill you." From this quotation alone, it's clear that Musk doesn't believe in taking time off. Instead, he prefers that his employees are as efficient as possible.

Perhaps this is why the entrepreneur found himself embroiled in conflict in 2015. *Elon Musk: Tesla, SpaceX, and the Quest for a Fantastic Future*, a novel published that year by author Ashlee Vance, details a disturbing anecdote about Musk's demanding nature. Specifically, the novel tells the story of longtime Musk assistant Mary Beth Brown. Brown, who had worked for Musk for twelve years, was reportedly put on leave when asking for a raise.

Musk's reasoning? He believed that Mary Beth Brown should first prove her worth to the company before receiving any additional compensation. As such, he reportedly required her to take a two-week vacation in which he assumed her duties to find out whether or not she was truly critical to company operations.

Unfortunately for Brown, the genius decided no.

While the engineering genius denies that Brown's firing happened in this manner, saying instead that Brown was unable to handle the increasing complexity of the job, the story goes to show one thing: Musk can be monstrously demanding of his employees.

Of course, one could argue that it is precisely Musk's demanding nature that has led him to such massive success. And while that may be true to a large extent, it's important to realize that Musk's demanding nature has drawn criticism from a variety of talking heads in the business world and has potentially negatively influenced the lives of even loyal longtime employees.

- **Persistence**

Those who know Elon unanimously agree: the genius entrepreneur's ambitiousness often verges on fanaticism. Musk, who has publicly stated that the world cannot be changed on forty hours a week, is known to dedicate hours to his work. According to some, when Musk latches onto an idea, it can be hard to shake him away from it.

More importantly, Musk has a pre-planned vision of what he wants, and he is willing to work to get it. In fact, it's frustrating for Musk when others don't actively seek the same ends or with the same fervor. Musk made the rounds when he suggested in a company memo that employees who don't have anything to contribute to meetings should not even bother to come.

For Musk, then, it's imperative that he and everyone around him stay concentrated on both the work ahead and the bigger picture. Still, Musk's persistence to carry out even the most outlandish of his goals has created some issues for the entrepreneur.

Specifically, Musk's attraction to "science fiction" goals can be off-putting for some investors who doubt the feasibility of Musk's plans. Essentially, the problem lies in the fact that Musk remains hyper-committed to goals that are hard to get off the ground.

This can be seen in projects such as the Hyperloop and The Boring Company, which despite niche support, have largely been unable to attract serious investment. Musk's supporters will point to the fact that revolutionizing transportation takes time and that Musk has already proven with SpaceX that persistence pays off.

While this is undeniably true, it's worth noting that Musk has spent considerable resources on the development of projects such as The Boring Company and Neuralink that have yet to produce large-scale results.

For Musk, this means only one thing: his persistence to pursue sci-fi-like goals comes with a price. While it's true that Musk's efforts could likely revolutionize transportation and the world we live in in a few years, it's also clear that Musk's image as a "Tony Stark" figure makes it difficult for some investors to take him or his projects seriously.

- **Self-Centered**

According to some, Musk also embodies strong self-centeredness that can be off-putting at times. While being the CEO of companies like Tesla and SpaceX is certainly something to brag about—and while having over ninety-four billion dollars is a feat that a majority of the world's population will never come close to achieving—some would make the case that the genius's confidence verges on hubris.

Unfortunately, this egotism has caused rifts between Musk and those he cares about—particularly on the home front.

When speaking about Elon, ex-wife Justine Wilson recalled an unusual moment from their wedding day. As the celebrations raged on around them, Elon came close and allegedly whispered in her ear, "I am the alpha in this relationship." According to Wilson, this comment would set the tone for their marriage, which would eventually end in divorce.

Wilson attributes their divorce to Elon's overbearing nature and inability to think past himself. Of Elon, she stated, "He does what he wants, and he is relentless about it." In essence, Musk does what he wants, when he wants, and it doesn't matter what anyone else thinks.

Wilson also had this to say, "It's Elon's world, and the rest of us are just living in it."

It's evident that Musk's inability to consider other viewpoints has led to some strife at home. With three divorces in the books, Musk has found it difficult to settle down into a long-term relationship. Part of this, no doubt, results from his ego.

Ex-wife Justine Wilson made it clear that Musk sees himself as superior to others. Recalling an argument she once had with her husband, she states that Elon told her, "If you were my employee, I would fire you."

Second wife Talulah Riley echoed Wilson's sentiments, stating that Musk's ambitions drove her away and made marriage with Elon "…quite the crazy ride."

For Musk, who has gone on the record stating, "I will never be happy without having someone. Going to sleep alone kills me," it's clear that hubris has had a detrimental impact on the genius engineer's life.

As you can see, many of Musk's negative traits aren't inherently negative. In fact, quite a few of them can be viewed as key factors in his success. Traits such as being demanding and persistent help the entrepreneur to stay on track and grow his organizations—though some would argue that he embodies these qualities to the extreme.

For this reason, it could be argued that the entrepreneur's true fault is extremism. For Musk, everything operates in overdrive. In other words, the entrepreneur's work ethic and drive to succeed far out shadow those of his employees and the people surrounding him.

In short, Musk's extremism and commitment to his goals can be off-putting for both potential employees and investors alike. This highlights the need to view Musk as a flawed character who, despite his shortcomings, is working hard to revolutionize the world we live in.

Bad Habits

It's not just his bad traits, however, that have gotten Musk into trouble over the course of his career. The serial entrepreneur has increasingly involved himself in controversy through persistent bad habits. These habits have hurt Musk's image in the eyes of some in the business community, despite arguably being one of the main reasons the genius engineer has developed such a large online following.

Let's take a look at some of Musk's worst habits and see what role they play in defining his career.

- **Twitter Storms**

Like other high-profile celebrities, Musk often takes to Twitter to voice his frustrations and rant about what he thinks is important. Unfortunately for Musk, his constant Twitter use has come with its own share of problems.

Specifically, many see his "irresponsible" use of Twitter as hurting the Tesla brand and his own stock. He has already faced contempt of court charges for breaking a settlement agreed upon in a 2018 lawsuit. Musk, who disclosed material information about Tesla via Twitter without clearing it first with his lawyer, had again come under judicial scrutiny.

The serial entrepreneur is known to use his Twitter account as an extension of his personal and professional brands. It has been through Twitter that Musk has been able to amass a large following that goes beyond his normal consumer base. Simply put, the platform has helped enable the serial entrepreneur to develop a strong personal brand.

Despite this, the "everything-goes" attitude that Musk displays on Twitter is often the opposite of what one would expect from a CEO. Musk has used the platform to post outrageous claims about his companies and his products' potential.

Arguably even worse, however, the serial entrepreneur has used Twitter to rag on individuals with whom he has disagreements. Notably, Musk made headlines when he called Vernon Unsworth, an expert cave explorer who rescued a youth soccer team from near-death in a Thai cave, a pedophile. The claim, which was made baselessly and without any substantiation, drew large amounts of criticism from those outside of Musk's immediate circle.

The behavior, they said, was not fitting of a CEO and could potentially damage Musk's stocks. Seeming to realize this, Musk issued an apology—but only after Unsworth threatened legal action against the genius. Unfortunately, the genius engineer, whose initial Tweet read,

"Sorry pedo guy, you really did ask for it," never backed away from his claims.

Unsworth sued Musk for defamation and sought $190 million in damages. The decision was left to jurors, and they unanimously concluded that Unsworth and his legal team were not able to prove their case as it lacked evidence.

Musk won, but the original Twitter thread has since been deleted; he would later go on to question why Unsworth never explicitly denied the claim that he was a pedophile.

Statements such as this have led Musk observers to wonder if he's begun to cripple under the pressure of leading two world-leading companies in Tesla and SpaceX. With Musk's Twitter behavior becoming more erratic and personal, journalists have started to question the serial entrepreneur's ability to cope with stress and manage his EQ (emotional quotient).

In short, Musk's use of Twitter has landed him in a ton of trouble. Fortunately, perhaps the events of 2018-19—which have seen Musk get himself embroiled in a federal lawsuit and face potential slander charges because of his Twitter use—have caused the serial entrepreneur to reevaluate his use of the platform. In a statement, he said, "I have made the mistaken assumption—and I will attempt to be better at this—of thinking that because somebody is on Twitter and is attacking me that it is open season. And that is my mistake. I will correct it."

- **Bad PR**

For a brilliant CEO of some of the world's hottest corporations, one would imagine that Musk would keep a straight-faced image. After all, this is the mold that has been handed down by other tech innovators such as Bill Gates, Steve Jobs, and other high-profile CEOs.

Unfortunately, Musk seems to have a knack for involving himself in controversies—and not just on Twitter. The serial entrepreneur can't seem to avoid sticking his fingers on a hot stove. From lambasting users and individuals online to smoking weed on live video podcasts (which we'll discuss in greater length later), Musk continuously involves himself in PR situations that most CEOs seek to avoid.

Musk's bad PR results from an inability to balance two opposing responsibilities: the necessity to lead Tesla and his other corporations confidently and boldly into the future and the desire to interact with a growing number of fans have latched onto his personal brand.

Both are essential to Musk's future success—but these two goals are not always directly aligned. For this reason, Musk has found it difficult to stay away from potential PR issues. Simply put, what riles up the masses on Twitter may not be what's best for Tesla shareholders, who wish to see a responsible Musk make responsible decisions online.

For this reason, it's worth viewing Musk's relationship with his fans, his corporations, and the media in the greater context. With so much to balance, it's no wonder that the serial entrepreneur frequently finds himself in controversy. Still, it's undeniable that his inability to completely balance his professional responsibilities has led to a number of personal and business problems.

In order to correct these issues, it's imperative that Musk finds a way to appeal to his large and growing base in a way that doesn't damage PR.

- **Fighting with Media**

In the era of fake news, genius engineer-entrepreneur Elon Musk has oft been compared to President Donald Trump—a characterization he calls predictable and low resolution.

The comparisons come in the way that Musk has handled himself in front of the media. Over the years, his relationship with media and news outlets has proven to be strained at best, with Elon often squabbling with journalists.

Perhaps this rocky relationship culminated with Musk stating that he wished to create a website that would track journalists' stories and provide them with an overall credibility rating. It came after the entrepreneur questioned the honesty of news media organizations.

For many, such comments harkened back to President Donald Trump's repeated claims of fake news and media dishonesty. It's a comparison that Musk himself may not be too fond of, as he has gone on record in disagreeing with many of the President's policies.

Most notably, Musk criticized the President's decision to pull out of the Paris Climate Accord, a move that went against Musk's eco-friendly beliefs.

Still, however, the comparisons remain—and Musk's assertions that he'd create a website ranking journalists' credibility does nothing to distance himself from them.

How much of this remains justifiable, however? Could it be true, as has been proven so many times over the last three years, that the media is, in fact operating with an agenda? Could Musk's comments about media dishonesty say more about the media than about any connection that draws between him and the President?

An objective look at the media's behavior and accuracy over the past few years may, indeed, prove Musk correct. And though it may not look the best for his companies for him to stay engaged in media disputes, one certainly can't be faulted for telling the truth.

- **Overselling**

The bigger problems come when Musk manages to oversell the truth. It appears to be something that the serial entrepreneur does out of habit without even realizing it.

One may say that he speaks with hyperbolic language. Or it may simply be that he proves to be such a visionary that he sees his dreams as being true.

For the rest of the world, however, the rhetoric can prove to be a bit much at times. Take, for instance, the case of a man whose overreliance on Tesla's self-driving technology cost him his life. The man, Joshua Brown, was reportedly watching *Harry Potter* clips while going down the road. In doing so, he failed to pay attention to the road—and his car's technology failed to notice the brightly-lit side of a white semi-truck.

This resulted in a fatal crash that cost Brown his life. Some have attributed such cases to the rhetoric of Musk. They state that Elon has failed to adequately inform people about the capabilities of his self-driving cars and instead paints an image of them being infallible.

It's something they believe has caused individuals like Brown to lose their lives for depending too much on the car's technology. Because they believed it was more secure and advanced than it really was, they failed to adequately pay attention to the road.

In all fairness here, however, one may just as easily say that Musk's words have no real impact in such situations. It can be argued, for instance, that it's the driver's responsibility to make sure that they're following safe practices on the road—no matter the car that they're in.

The issue proves controversial all around, however, and it seems as though Musk is addressing it the best way he knows how: by creating increasingly dependable and technologically-advanced self-driving cars.

Bad History

Unfortunately, Musk has more than just a few bad traits. The Tesla CEO has earned a less-than-stellar history—one that has landed him in serious legal trouble in the past.

As we'll see, the range of bad behaviors that Musk has committed reaches from minor misconduct to illegal and fraudulent behavior.

- **Dropped Out of School**

When examining Musk's history, it can be difficult at times to determine if he did something wrong. Why?

Because the results usually turn out to be good anyway. Consider, for example, his decision to drop out of Stanford's PhD program. Such a move goes against everything most people have ever been taught about getting an education.

That's not to say, however, that it didn't work for Musk. The forward-thinking entrepreneur was able to use this to his advantage and make his first multi-million-dollar project. The problem, then, comes with millions of Musk fans wondering if they would be able to do the same—when the truth is that Musk capitalized on a very specific set of circumstances that may not exist for everyone.

It also becomes a bad part of his history when one considers that Musk dropping out of school is a much more famous notion than him attending it. In other words, most people buy into the myth that Musk never attended any schooling at all and that he instead became a CEO and product architect of Tesla, Inc.

This myth, however, remains unsupported by reality, as Musk holds a double degree from the University of Pennsylvania. For this reason, those who wish to follow in Musk's footsteps and drop out of school altogether and pursue entrepreneurial endeavors may not achieve the same results.

Musk's willingness to accept such a large risk when dropping out of Stanford may not seem like a bad thing. But that's only because it worked. What happens when others try, and it doesn't work for them?

The lesson here isn't so clear. Perhaps the strongest justification of Musk is that the entrepreneur was able to read the market—and that he doesn't control what myths others believe about him. Musk, himself, doesn't encourage his followers to drop out of school, and anyone who holds this belief misunderstands his history. In this way, though the action he committed may not have been bad, public perception has turned it into something that could be damaging for many people in society.

But, really, can Musk be blamed for that? Probably not.

- **Smoking Weed on Podcast**

What he can be blamed for, however, is smoking weed on the Joe Rogan Podcast. This move incensed a number of people, including others in the business community.

The reason was simple: Musk managed to get away with doing something that many of his followers, indeed his employees, would never be able to pull off.

Musk's naysayers note that had his employees showed up to work smoking weed or with it in their systems, they likely would have been fired. This reflected an obvious double standard that favored the serial entrepreneur and put him on a pedestal.

Even more troubling for many of these were allegations that Musk's behavior represented a form of racial privilege. African-American activists took the time to note their belief that African-Americans are over-prosecuted for similar offenses and that Musk's ability to get away with smoking weed in public only reflected a form of systemic privilege.

It's hard to defend Musk's actions in this case—as he performed a blatantly illegal action in public. What's more, he seemed to care little about it after the fact, never expressing regret for the incident.

This has led some to question just how Musk sees himself and what attitudes he may have. Additionally, the hypocrisy of the situation doesn't create the best image for Musk's character.

Nor for his business. Many were quick to note that the unprofessional image that Musk created while smoking wasn't one that would do him any favors. With other businesses potentially wanting to distance themselves from the backlash that his weed smoking caused, Musk did more than incense viewers.

He potentially cost his company lucrative deals. In this way, Musk's actions created somewhat of a bad press storm for his companies and worked to undermine the professional image he's worked so hard to establish. Considering the fact that many of Musk's companies have off-the-wall goals, it's important that they maintain as professional an image as possible. Without some form of credibility, they may not be able to secure the deals and funding they need.

What's even worse, as we will see, is that Musk's actions came amid a growing scandal with the SEC—causing some to wonder just how much the CEO cared for the future of his companies.

A Bigger History?

Additionally, many have wondered if Musk's actions represented a part of a larger history of drug abuse. Many individuals claim, for instance, that the serial entrepreneur has a long-standing history with other forms of psychedelic drugs.

In particular, rumors note that Elon holds parties where he buys and uses LSD. While these rumors have remained unsubstantiated, as we'll see, if they're true, they could be playing a large role in how he has been conducting himself in the public image.

Especially on Twitter.

So, where's the silver lining for Musk here? Many of his defenders are quick to note that LSD usage is nothing more than a rumor. Additionally, they point to the growing legalization of marijuana across the country, calling it a normal action that most Americans are starting to support. In this regard, they see Musk as trailblazing another path yet again. In their mind, Musk's smoking didn't reflect a hypocritical double standard. Instead, it worked to show that even the most successful individuals can and do smoke weed, helping further the case that it should be legalized.

- **Lied about Investments**

Perhaps Musk's biggest flaw so far has been in his inability, to tell the truth online. While this may seem to be a small deal, it's actually landed the serial entrepreneur in serious legal trouble.

The Securities & Exchange Commission (SEC) tried Musk for contempt of court in April 2019, leading to the future of Musk's involvement with his businesses remaining in limbo—all for actions that he could have controlled.

The drama started in 2018 when Musk was accused of providing false information to drive up stock prices for Tesla. Taking to Twitter, Musk noted that he had secured funding to take Tesla private, and the stocks would be only $420 a share.

The news sent a ripple through the investment community, with many willing to bite on the seemingly-great deal. It also raised questions about the certainty of funding and where it would come from.

There was only one problem.

Musk never did secure the funding. In this way, the serial entrepreneur's actions served to be fraudulent behavior in the eyes of the SEC, landing Musk and Tesla in serious trouble. Following a fine and a court order not to tweet again without approval, Musk returned as CEO of Tesla.

It wasn't long before rumors that Musk was on LSD during his initial tweeting binge started to circulate. Fueled by actress Azealia Banks, who claimed to have been with Musk at the time, the rumors cast doubt on Musk's ability to professionally manage his Twitter.

Unfortunately, these doubts soon proved to be true, with Musk once again taking to Twitter in February of 2019 with yet another controversial post. This time, Musk gave highly-inflated estimates for the number of cars Tesla looked to produce in 2019. The SEC and others took this to represent another case in which Musk fudged the numbers to dupe investors—a claim that Musk and his legal team have denied.

However, a larger problem emerged from this scandal when it was shown that Musk had violated court orders to seek permission before tweeting. Calling it a violation of his First Amendment Freedoms, Musk decided to challenge the SEC over contempt of court charges in early April.

According to Musk, his settlement with SEC only required him to seek approval of Tweets that are relevant to shareholders. He further said that the vehicle production tweet did not meet that criterion and was a violation of his First Amendment Freedoms.

The SEC did not take this lightly and fired back. They said, "Musk's contention — that the potential size of a car company's production for the year could not reasonably be material — borders on the ridiculous," the agency said. "Musk's shifting justifications [for tweeting the projection without approval] suggest that there was never any good-faith effort to comply with the Court's order and the Tesla Policy. Rather, Musk has simply elected to ignore them."

Such arguments kept taking place until finally, the matter was settled with the removal of Musk from his post as chairman of Tesla and a $20 million fine. Of course, none of this has stopped Musk from tweeting what he wants to.

Why, then, does Musk continue to defy orders and tweet misleading statistics? For his part, Musk notes that his tweets were misinterpreted. His initial tweet promising $420 a share, he says, was intended as a marijuana joke, playing on the number 420. So far, however, no one is laughing.

Is there anything redeeming in this for Musk? For starters, one must remember to separate rumors from facts. Additionally, in this case, one must also look to separate any intention from his wrongdoings. Could it not, perhaps, be true that Musk simply made a poor joke—something we've all been guilty of at some point in our lives? Were the follow-up tweets nothing more than an error that Musk quickly managed to correct?

It's likely going to be up to the courts to decide. However, one may predict that following this ordeal; Musk will likely tone down his controversial online presence, although that is a bleak possibility.

The Bigger Picture

Clearly, Musk isn't the saint that many of his fans likely want him to be. Despite his flaws, however, the genius has put together one of the most impressive resumes and reputations in the modern era.

When judging Musk's history of misdeeds, it's important that one keep perspective. No one is immune to making mistakes—not even Musk—and it's likely that his flaws are blown out of proportion. This often happens to those in the limelight—especially those like Musk, who work to break established norms.

In judging Musk's moral success, then, one must keep in mind the bigger picture that's always at play. Through his work over the last decade, Musk has managed to make several important technological leaps. Not only that, his efforts to create a more environmentally-friendly world have helped make it a better place for both humans and animals.

Importantly, in this regard, Musk's revolutionary work seeks to improve the standard of living for citizens across the globe. One must also not ignore the amazing technological contributions that Musk has given to the world.

In this light, the mistakes that Musk has made over the course of his career begin to seem inconsequential. Though certainly, no one is immune to the consequences of their actions, keep in mind the full body of one's moral work before passing judgment.

Additionally, remember that Musk has faced his fair share of consequences, just like the rest of us. With his Twitter storms now landing him in court, Musk has been held accountable for his mistakes.

In this way, it may be more beneficial to stay trained on the serial entrepreneur's good work as a society. By focusing on the powerful technological advancements that Musk has continually developed and promised, it may be that we can more quickly advance as a nation and as a society.

With this in mind, it's important not to excuse Musk's misgivings nor dwell on them, either. Instead, by accepting Musk as a human who has flaws, we'll be better situated to support Musk in his life-changing endeavors. By coming together this way, we can help change the future for people across the globe.

Elon Musk and COVID-19

The COVID-19 pandemic has created havoc in all major countries of the world. The disease caused by a virus has put everyone on fire. It has left none behind, not even the developed countries with super-advanced medical facilities. In response to its uncontrollable spread, many countries, including the US, have taken strong steps, including a "lockdown," to reduce the critical consequences of this crisis. However, forcing people to act according to the government's will is against the freedom of citizenship, which is what a few have to say about the lockdown situation. Tesla and SpaceX founder Elon Musk has similar views. He believes that the way the United States is handling the lockdown scenario during the COVID-19 pandemic is not democratic. Rather, he calls it a "fascist act." He considers it a violation of citizens' constitutional rights to cage them in their own homes. Though authorities declared that lockdown is to slow down the speed of its spread, Musk argues that it is an authoritarian expression to stab the personal freedom everyone should have the right to.

While the lockdown affirms the orders for everyone to stay at home, Musk blames the government for its "horrible" and "wrong" ways of dealing with the situation. The US is the symbol of freedom, and in a call with investors, Musk mentioned that abandoning personal freedom itself wipes out the basic intention of building America. "This is not why people came to this country," he says.

In terms of industrial economics, Elon Musk shares that the lockdown will undoubtedly have a huge negative impact on not just Tesla but all companies in the US, many of which will not survive through this. As per Musk, working from home should be an allowance, not a compulsion.

On the other hand, his contemporaries are not so sure of reopening the nation so early. Facebook founder Mark Zuckerberg expressed worries about the infection rates and their future impacts on longer-term health and economic conditions. Facebook's response to the pandemic was clear from a major step taken to cancel all in-person meetings with more than 50 people until June 2021.

However, Musk argued against the lockdown and asked the state, through Twitter, to give people's freedom back to them. He seems to appreciate Texas's steps in releasing the restrictions related to lockdown. In other tweets, he suggests that authorities come up with other solutions of reopening businesses with more care and appropriate protective measures instead of forcing compulsory house-arrest on everybody.

Yet it might be evident from his tweet on March 19, 2020 that Musk has underestimated the disastrous impact of COVID-19. In that tweet, he indicates a probability of "close to zero new cases" in America by the end of April, which certainly did not come true, with the increasing number of patients. Musk himself suffered and recovered from a COVID-19 infection in November 2020. So, you can be wild as you can in guessing what his next COVID tweet will predict.

SECTION 4
ELON MUSK—MYTHS
AND FAILURES

CHAPTER ONE

MYTHS ABOUT ELON MUSK

Introduction

Elon Musk is one of the most successful entrepreneurs and colorful personalities of our time. With his visionary companies and eccentric ideas, the serial entrepreneur has inspired millions of people across the world. In many ways, Musk proves more than just a cultural icon. Indeed, the serial entrepreneur has become the stuff of legend.

For this reason, it can often be difficult to separate man from myth when it comes to Elon Musk. Due to his success, Musk is often viewed as "superhuman" by his followers, and oftentimes he seems more like a comic book character than a real-life human being.

Because of this, it's important to find out what's true and what's not concerning Elon Musk. In doing so, you may find that you have just what it takes to be like the visionary serial entrepreneur. In this post, we'll distinguish myth from reality and set the record straight on just who Elon Musk really is.

Let's begin!

1. He Has a Photographic Memory

One of the most persistent myths about Elon Musk is that he has a photographic memory. We're not sure where this myth started, but we've seen it touted across the web. Some of his most die-hard supporters claim that he's able to remember specific details of everything he reads—proving that he has a photographic memory. For reference, a photographic memory entails that an individual can remember events, faces, and details with true photographic clarity.

In the context of Elon Musk, this means that the genius remembers just about everything he sees or reads.

While there's no doubt that Musk has an extraordinary memory, the truth of the matter is that the concept of a "photographic memory" has never been proven. In an article in the *Scientific American*, Barry Gordon, professor of neurology at John Hopkins School of Medicine, states that "Even visual memories that are close to the photographic ideal are far from truly photographic."

What does this mean? Simply put, it means that Elon Musk, the genius founder of SpaceX and Tesla CEO, likely does not have a photographic memory—even if he does possess above-average cognitive abilities. So why is this myth so popular? How can Musk supporters, who generally regard themselves as scientific and forward-thinking, take a seemingly anti-science stance when it comes to the eccentric serial entrepreneur?

There are a few reasons. Notably, Musk is said to have read the entire *Encyclopedia Britannica* at the age of nine. While that doesn't prove he has a photographic memory, it does show his intelligence and a commitment to knowledge.

What's more, it's been reported that Musk doesn't take notes in any of his Tesla or SpaceX meetings. Instead, the engineering genius is able to recall "thousands" of details and implement them with high precision—even days after the fact. When you're the CEO of several different startups and internationally-acclaimed corporations, that's a pretty big deal.

Still, none of this is evidence that Musk has anything close to a "photographic memory." In fact, it's much more likely that Musk possesses above-average cognitive skills and brings unrivaled passion to his work. With this formula, it is quite easy to remember details at a high level.

This means that you, too, can follow Musk's example. Don't fall into the trap of thinking that you need something like a "photographic memory" to make an impact. The truth is that you just need to stay committed. Like Musk, if you become well-versed on any subject and stay passionate about it, you can easily bring more efficiency to any task you set out to do.

2. He is a "Real-Life Tony Stark"

Now that we've busted the myth of the "photographic memory," let's turn to a myth that's even more widespread. In fact, you've likely heard this one before. If you read any column on the serial entrepreneur, you'll see Musk called a "real-life Tony Stark."

But how accurate is this moniker? Better yet, was Elon Musk really the basis for the world-famous Marvel character Tony Stark (aka Iron Man)?

Well, yes and no. Let's look at each of these questions in turn. If you've never seen Iron Man, simply know that Tony Stark is an eccentric genius who forays into the realm of experimental AI and space technology.

Understandably, on the surface, this does sound quite a lot like Musk. In fact, there are a number of similarities that may seem stunning at a glance. Specifically, both men have a degree in physics, have helped create revolutionary technology, followed after the professions of their fathers, and are interested in space technology. Still, there are a number of differences between the two successful and genius entrepreneurs.

Most notably, one is a superhero, and one is not. And while you can draw a shallow parallel between Stark, who flies around in his Iron

Man suit and saves the world from trouble, and Musk, whose involvement in clean energy, electric cars, and human-friendly AI seeks to stabilize the future of humanity, the similarities truly end there.

Knowing this, let's tackle another issue. Many claim that Tony Stark was actually based off Elon Musk. However, closer inspection of this myth causes it to fall apart. In reality, Stan Lee based his 1963-character, Tony Stark, after another billionaire business magnate: Howard Hughes.

In an interview, Lee stated, "Howard Hughes was one of the most colorful men of our time. He was an inventor, an adventurer, a multi-billionaire, a ladies' man, and finally a nutcase."

A quick survey of the *Iron Man* comics or films shows that this description fits the bill of Tony Stark pretty nicely. Still, it appears Elon Musk did have some involvement in the development of Robert Downey Jr.'s on-screen *Iron Man* character.

Leading up to the 2008 filming of the blockbuster *Iron Man* film, Downey Jr. asked producers if he could sit down with Elon Musk, a man he thought resembled Tony Stark. Reportedly, the two met, and Stark based many of his quirks and mannerisms off the Tesla Founder.

While this is an interesting tidbit, it's perhaps too much to say that the two are interchangeable. In fact, with a level of dedication, it's possible that most of us can resemble the two men, as well. While that doesn't mean we will be billionaires or have virtually infinite resources at our disposal, it does suggest that we can do our best to save the world from harm, environmental or otherwise. We can also follow after the two men and look toward the future, constantly thinking of ways to improve our surroundings and the lives of others.

Perhaps the goal shouldn't be to paint Musk as some "superhuman" figure but instead, embrace his good qualities and try to embody them in our own actions and daily lives.

3. He Has the Answer to Everything

Speaking of "superhuman," this leads us to our next point. Some Internet superfans believe that Musk has the answer to everything. These days, Musk has become a cultural phenomenon; YouTube videos involving Musk garner millions of views in just a matter of days. Internet websites like Quora are full of questions regarding Musk's views on a variety of issues from astrobiology to the future and viability of cryptocurrency.

At times, it feels like Musk is expected to have the answer to everything. And we get it. After helping revolutionize the automobile industry and founding one of the world's leading private space companies, Musk has set himself up as a scientific authority. Still, it often seems as if people forget that Musk is still human.

We love Elon Musk as next as the next person—and admire him for the work he's done for the planet and for the scientific community—but we believe it's important to recognize that no one has the answer to everything. As such, a rabid belief in anything the genius says probably isn't the way to go.

What's for sure is that Musk is rapidly changing the face of the Earth with his electric cars and making the future of space travel much more interesting with his Mars-bound rocket ships. In areas of his expertise, Musk can be considered one of the world's foremost authorities.

Still, too often, we get the impression that Musk simply works alone. The truth of the matter is that there are teams of individuals at each of Musk's companies who help in the development of the serial entrepreneur's technology. And while Musk does oversee each of his projects personally, let's not mistake that as meaning that Musk does all his work by himself.

In fact, it could be said that Musk benefits from surrounding himself with highly qualified people. For his company OpenAI, the genius entrepreneur has poached some of the world's leading authorities on the subject and the top AI developers in the game. For his Hyperloop project, Musk hosts several competitions that enable entrepreneurs from around the world to test out their own Hyperloop designs.

Obviously, this outside innovation goes a long way to the success that is "Elon Musk." So, what does this mean? In basic terms, it means that Elon Musk does not have the answer to everything. Some fans may take that as an insult—but what it truly means is that Musk, like the rest of us, is human.

An exceptional human, no doubt—but human.

This means that, as individuals, we should do more to emulate the serial entrepreneur. We could do so by staying committed to our goals and surrounding ourselves with people who allow us to succeed. Furthermore, like Musk, we should come at our work with unending dedication and tireless energy. In doing so, we could be doing a great service to the planet.

4. He Started Tesla

Perhaps the most common myth about Musk is that he "started" Tesla. Though Musk is the current CEO of Tesla and has received retroactive founding status, the reality is that the serial entrepreneur did not have a hand in the initial founding of Tesla.

So, what's the real story behind the multi-billion-dollar automobile company? The company was established in 2003 by Martin Eberhard (original and longtime CEO) and Marc Tarpenning. The two entrepreneurs had the notion to start the company after the failure of GM's E-V1, an electric car that was meant to signal in the new era of electric vehicles.

After the car's spectacular failure, the two men decided to capitalize on the empty space in the automobile industry to design an electric sports vehicle that could revolutionize the industry. They named their startup after the Serbian-American inventor Nikola Tesla.

So how does Musk fit into all this? Though the genius was not technically a Tesla founder, he did contribute $30 million of his own money to the startup and served as its first chairman starting in 2004. In 2008, the company released its first-ever vehicle, named the Roadster, to critical acclaim. At the time, the car was considered one of the best electric vehicles ever made, putting Tesla squarely on the map for the future of innovation.

Surprisingly, however, both original founders left the company the same year. This opened up space for Musk to eventually take over as CEO. Under Musk's leadership, the company has grown into the largest and bestselling electric automobile manufacturer in the world, with annual sales blowing out the competition.

What's more, with "green" companies such as SolarCity involved to make the brand even more environmentally friendly and sustainable, Tesla only looks to grow in the coming years. This means that, while not founder, Musk has taken the company to new and unprecedented heights.

What can we learn from Musk's example? Namely that you don't need to be the originator of an idea to take a concept to its highest level. Though the serial entrepreneur did not think of Tesla or its initial business strategy, it is his own genius that has helped the company become what it is today.

For the layman, this means that we could bring more value to the world by injecting our own personal ideas and values into the situations we are involved in. Simply put, you don't need to be a CEO to help change the world. Like Musk, you can work your way up and eventually define your own legacy.

5. He Thinks Ten Times More Quickly than the Average Man

There are many words to describe Elon Musk. The serial entrepreneur is "visionary," "eccentric," and, yes, "genius." This is evident in his education and in his ability to turn startups into gold. Still, is it true that the celebrated serial entrepreneur thinks "ten times more quickly than the average man," as some online superfans would have you believe?

Chances are, not really. Though Musk is undeniably smart, there's no need to put him on such a high pedestal. Doing so only unfairly props the serial entrepreneur up (making him more susceptible to criticism) and brings down your own individual self-worth.

The truth of the matter is that while Musk is smart, this isn't the most important quality he brings to the table. In fact, as CEO, he doesn't even need to be that smart. Simply put, Musk has access to some of the world's smartest people, meaning he has a nearly endless stream of intelligence at his disposal.

This is why his personal work ethic and unique mindset are much more important. Musk isn't afraid to think outside the box, and it's this type of innovation that is currently helping the serial entrepreneur shape the world.

Of course, however, he couldn't do any of this without bringing endless energy and passion to everything that he does. Musk ignores criticism and doesn't let anyone get in his way of following his dreams. This is undeniably true, as he has proved critics wrong time and again with companies such as Tesla and SpaceX (which will soon be sending crafts to Mars).

What does this mean? It's simple. It means that Musk's success has everything to do with his workaholic status and his drive to help people. The serial entrepreneur is where he is today because of his endless drive to make the world a better place.

In order to change the world, the rest of us should follow Musk's example. This means not being afraid to fail. In fact, Musk has had his own share of failures. Not only was he ousted from his CEO position during the early days of his career at X.com, but his SpaceX company has also seen some pretty nasty rocket crashes.

Still, the genius entrepreneur remains undeterred in bringing about a new vision for the world. This vision is based on a scientific need to make positive changes for our planet that can help aid in human survival and potentially make humans an interplanetary species.

Want to be like Elon Musk? The formula is simple, and you need more than just intelligence. You'll need undeterred passion, energy, and the commitment to work hard toward an ideal, even in the face of criticism. Following this formula can help all of us be a little more like Elon Musk.

6. He Started PayPal

Much of the wonder that surrounds Elon Musk may be unearned. Though the genius entrepreneur has earned quite the reputation, it's sometimes for things he didn't do.

For instance, Musk is often credited as starting PayPal. This myth comes from a misunderstanding of Musk's complicated involvement with the company.

It's worth keeping in mind that recognizing this myth for what it is helps put the serial entrepreneur in a new light. Many of his admirers wonder how one man could found so many companies—feeling that it's impossible for them to do the same.

However, as we've seen, Musk's involvement in different companies hasn't always been to the degree people believe.

Such is the case with PayPal.

Instead, Musk's foray into the online financial domain started with another company all of his own. Musk's company, known as X.com, offered basic financial services and email payments. Though it's true that Musk's X.com did fairly well, it was actually his rival—Confinity—that started the PayPal service we've come to know and love today.

After fierce competition between the two companies, Musk's X.com acquired Confinity. At this time, Musk now had direct control over Confinity's new project PayPal.

Here, it's important to note that Musk played an integral role in the early development of PayPal. He even went on to become one of the largest stakeholders in the company.

That being said; however, Musk's affair with PayPal was short-lived. He eventually found himself ousted from the CEO position over the company by other stakeholders who felt that he was too young.

Though rejected from his role of power, Musk remained one of the most prominent stakeholders in PayPal. This would later prove Musk's first major financial success, as eBay would eventually acquire PayPal in October of 2002.

When they did, Musk found that his significant stakes in PayPal made him very wealthy overnight. eBay's $1.5 billion acquisition of PayPal would make Musk one of the wealthiest men in the world—and it would start a new era for the online finance company.

Though Musk played a large role in the early development of PayPal, much of how we view the company today came after his involvement. It must also be noted that because Musk did not invent PayPal, he can't really be credited with it. At least not to the degree he is by some fans.

So, what does this mean?

In short, it means that while certainly a brilliant success, Musk's track record doesn't prove to be as superhuman as some would believe. Instead of creating nearly every major company under the sun, Musk has managed to bring his large skillset to the table in a variety of unique ways.

And, as we've noted, this comes from both his intelligence and his hard-working nature. By adopting a similar work pattern and using their own wit, aspiring entrepreneurs can achieve a similar level of success.

7. He is Vegan

Musk's personal brand image has evolved to be one that paints him in only the best of lights. Despite this, it appears that the genius engineer is sometimes credited with being more of a saint than he really is.

For example, many hold the belief that Musk is a vegan. This myth has been fueled, no doubt, by the fact that Musk has made a career out of environmental preservation.

Musk's work at SolarCity, for instance, looks to help in the drive for the development of renewable energy.

Most notably, however, his work at Tesla has made him one of the most well-known voices in the environmental protection arena.

Musk and his team at Tesla have created a variety of different electric cars that look to reduce man's carbon footprint.

Hailed for this planet-saving work, Musk has also been attributed with certain qualities that he simply doesn't have.

Case in point, Musk's desire to reduce carbon emissions stops short of his love for meat. Though many mistakenly believe that the eccentric serial entrepreneur avoids all animal products, Musk has gone on the record saying otherwise.

In fact, Musk has been quoted as saying that while he believes going vegan and vegetarian would help reduce man's carbon footprint; he simply can't bring himself to do it.

So, what is that has fueled this myth?

Even more, why does it matter?

For starters, the vegan Elon Musk myth may stem from more than just Musk's glowing environmental track record.

He's also had a few glowing words to say about veganism during his time at SpaceX.

"I'm a big fan of free choice for any future Martian colony," he said, in an interview with Space.com. "That said, it is likely that early Mars colonists would have a mostly vegetable diet, because of the energy and space needed to raise farm animals."

The comment even drew a response from PETA, reflecting just how far-reaching Musk's comments can be.

The myth likely also received some reinforcement in 2016, when it was reported that Tesla was "going vegan."

At the time, Musk's electric car company looked to step things up by ditching leather as a material used to make seats in their cars. Instead, Musk looked to add a vegan-friendly alternative.

As reported, prior to the 2016 announcement, Tesla only offered vegan-friendly seats for those who custom ordered them.

The move to drop leather as a material no doubt hearkens back to Musk's goal of reducing carbon emissions—and it no doubt furthered the view that the Tesla CEO himself is vegan.

Even if he's not vegan, you may wonder, how does this apply to you? Why does it matter if Musk is a vegan, vegetarian, or a meat-eater?

For starters, debunking this myth goes a long way to show that you can help a cause without actually living it yourself. While it certainly can't be denied that Musk is doing more than just about everyone on the planet in terms of eco-friendly innovations, it's also true that he doesn't apply this to every segment of his life.

For this reason, by understanding this, aspiring entrepreneurs can learn to apply a similar dedication to their passions—even if they don't stack up all the way. In other words, by realizing that Musk's commitment to reducing carbon emissions has been achieved through his hard work and not superhuman moral diligence, others can learn to follow in the serial entrepreneur's footsteps.

8. He Dropped Out of College

The origins of this myth aren't difficult to spot. That's because, in some ways, this myth actually proves true.

Elon Musk did drop out of college—but it may not be exactly what you think.

Musk first attended Queen's University in Canada in 1989. Musk, who was only seventeen at the time, did so in order to avoid compulsory military service in his home country of South Africa.

It's been reported; however, that Musk had no real intention of settling down in Canada. Instead, he used it as a springboard to gain citizenship to the United States.

While Musk didn't stick around Queen's University for more than three years, he did make some life-changing decisions there. For instance, it was at Queen's University that he met his first wife—with whom he would go on to have his children.

It could be that this Elon Musk rumor draws from the fact that he left Queen's University before graduating in 1992. It must be noted, however, that he did not completely withdraw from the university.

Instead, a hard-working Musk gained admittance into the University of Pennsylvania in 1992. It's here that this myth begins to fall apart—as Musk would go on to earn a bachelor's degree in economics.

In fact, the genius would do more than just earn a bachelor's degree during his time at Penn.

He would earn two.

Musk's second bachelor's was a degree in physics. It's here that this Musk rumor likely gains most of its credibility.

After graduating from Penn with his second bachelor's, Musk famously applied and was accepted into Stanford.

Here, he intended to pursue a PhD in energy physics. Musk's admission for such a high-level program no doubt reflects his intelligence; however, it was his long-term vision that would eventually make him his billions.

For instance, Musk remains famous for dropping out of Stanford to pursue a career as an entrepreneur. Hoping to build off the Internet boom, Musk went on to capitalize on various resources to become the engineering genius we know today.

So, is it true that Musk dropped out of college? Yes and no. While he didn't finish his doctoral degree in energy physics, he did earn two bachelor's degrees at the University of Pennsylvania.

What does this mean for you?

It may depend on how you look at it. While many Musk supporters have used this rumor to justify not attending college, that may be only half the story.

The real takeaway comes when realizing that Musk's success comes as a result of both his education and his long-term vision. While Musk did decide to drop out of his PhD program, he also thought it important enough to get two bachelor's degrees—both of which have no doubt helped him become successful today.

For the budding entrepreneur, this holds several lessons. First, make sure to have the proper education to take advantage of the opportunities available, and second, don't be afraid to take risks when opportunities arrive.

By incorporating these lessons from Elon Musk into your own strategy, you can start enjoying the greater entrepreneurial success of your own.

9. He is "Crazy"

Elon Musk has long been deemed eccentric—and even crazy. Smoking marijuana live on the Joe Rogan podcast in late 2018 did nothing to help the serial entrepreneur's image in this regard.

But what's the truth behind Musk's madness?

It may be hard to know. Though he certainly may fit the bill as being "eccentric," it's difficult to imagine a man of Musk's success being "crazy."

Worth over an astounding $94 billion, Musk's far-reaching visions have made him one of the wealthiest individuals on the planet. However, it's this same vision that has earned him the label of being just a bit looney.

This criticism of Musk extends from a variety of different factors. For instance, many in the scientific community scoff at the serial entrepreneur's predictions that commercial travel to Mars will soon be possible. Others have called his goals with Tesla nothing more than a pipedream.

None of this, however, has deterred Musk. Though one cannot deny the seeming implausibility of his goals, the success of his companies also can't be ignored.

His SpaceX company, for instance, became the first private company to pull off a number of difficult space endeavors. Since then, they've received official contracts from NASA to man crews and deliver cargo to the international space station.

Just a decade ago, this level of success would have been unheard of for a private space company. Since that time, however, Musk had grown to fill the gap that a depleted NASA left in its wake.

But Musk's legacy doesn't stop there. Following the failure of electric cars by GM, many figured that they were an impossibility.

Now, Tesla has some of the best-selling electric cars on the market. And these models are selling quickly, as a growing number of consumers are interested in Musk's environmentally-friendly options.

In this way, it can be said that the idea that Musk is crazy is nothing more than a myth. Though the serial entrepreneur has set an incredible amount of high goals, he has also delivered on many of them, beating expectations along the way.

Understanding this is important for all entrepreneurs. Musk's unwavering commitment to his goals despite criticism has made him one of the most successful businessmen on the planet.

By adopting a similar attitude, you too can start achieving your goals. By surrounding yourself with spirited team players with great ability—much as Musk does across the board at all of his companies—you can start working to make your dreams a reality.

10. Elon Musk Is Just a Famous "Personality"

Finally, this last myth may be one of the most vicious and common of all.

Many, who are likely jealous of Musk's success, note that he hasn't gotten famous through his hard work or vision at all. Instead, they say, he's become more of a personal brand legend than anything.

It's through this, they argue, that Musk has been able to build a vast empire and fortune.

Under close scrutiny, however, this theory falls apart. Though it's in no doubt fueled by some financial setbacks faced by Musk and some of his companies, a detailed look reveals it doesn't hold weight.

So, where does it come from?

It results from two driving factors.

One, many note that Musk takes credit for the work of others. We've seen, in small degrees, how this has played out over the years. However, this typically comes from the public's misconceptions about Musk's achievements and not by claims that he's made himself.

They also say that despite being CEO of so many companies, Musk has little to do with their innovations and designs. While harder to refute, this claim doesn't hold up when looking at the papers. For instance, Musk remains the lead designer of all projects with many of his companies.

More important; however, they argue that Musk and his companies wouldn't be anywhere without government money. His companies have been kept afloat, they argue, by government subsidies and contracts.

While this may be true to a certain extent, it speaks more to Musk's business prowess than to diminish it. By leveraging all possible funds that he can get, Musk has managed to run and make prosperous a number of different companies—of which he owns several different types.

Musk's ability to secure government funds and contracts reveals his business-savvy nature—showcasing that he's more than just a name.

In fact, Musk has milked these contracts to the tune of over $20 billion—all while creating some of the most important technological innovations of our time.

This goes to show that anyone with the right business plan and strategy can work their companies up to a great degree of prosperity. By avoiding the naysayers like Musk does, aspiring entrepreneurs can start to get their companies off the ground to reach higher levels of success.

The Bottom Line

Elon Musk has built one of the most impressive modern technological empires. Along with it has come a good bit of fame, a massive fortune, and a fair share of myths.

While these three factors have worked to create a mystic image of this genius engineer, it's important to keep perspective. By debunking the ten myths above, entrepreneurs can learn valuable business and life lessons from Musk. By having an accurate look at his career, these entrepreneurs can better learn how to guide their businesses for greater success.

Keep this information in mind as you look to emulate Musk's success.

Elon Musk's Stutter

One of the most common fears is public speaking. Many people tend to lose their confidence while talking because they feel that everybody is looking at them. This anxiety is part and parcel of a dialogue delivery to the audience. Elon Musk might be the most ambitious man in the world, as he is capable of doing so many things at a time. However, he fails at giving good public presentations. With his visionary direction, he has left no stone unturned; he is reframing space travel, focusing on electric auto vehicles, dreaming about digging a passage through Los Angeles, occupying Mars, etc.! There is no doubt about his proficiency at the minutest detail in the production of SpaceX Rockets and Tesla Motors. However, despite being the ace of everything mentioned above, he fumbles over his words when he is in front of a crowd.

Recently, a Twitter user shared a video of a press conference in 2011 where Musk is explaining the Falcon Heavy Rocket built by SpaceX. He is seen stammering during his speech. In response to this tweet, Elon expressed that he is not good at speaking in public. Earlier, many others had trolled Elon for his bad public speaking skills. A few of them even made a video about it. However, Elon fans pop up on social media to shower love and support on their hero. People admire him for his work more than his words. Their empathetic comments encourage him with regard to his nervousness about the stutter.

Even after getting pulled down morally by society, Elon has gone public wherever possible, notwithstanding his discomfort. He is aware that he is not a great orator, as he stutters and faces difficulty speaking fluently. However, he has faced his fears and kept moving ahead through the struggles. By accomplishing what he has been afraid of doing, he is an inspiration to all those who are willing to fight the battle in their minds. The moral of the story is: Get up, do what you are afraid to do, and rise above your apprehension. Keep going even if you fail and panic. Those who don't act upon the things that bother them will never succeed in becoming better.

CHAPTER TWO

BEING SUCCESSFUL IN SPITE OF FAILURES: THE ELON MUSK METHOD

If I told you to name one of the most frustrating experiences in life, failure would probably be number one on the list. Failure often makes us feel ashamed, and we feel like it's something we should hide.

What if I told you that the opposite is true? When we attempt great things, our failures speak as highly of us as our accomplishments. Don't believe me? Then let's take a look at what failure has meant to one of the most influential figures of the century; Elon Musk.

Elon Musk is one of the great geniuses, if not *the* genius of our time, and he's also the wealthiest person on the planet. What does this mean? This means he has accomplished many of the ideas he has pursued so far.

We can say without a doubt he has revolutionized and changed every industry he has put his hands on: the automotive industry with Tesla, sustainable energy with SolarCity, eCommerce with PayPal, and space flight and exploration with SpaceX.

But what do you think lies behind all these accomplishments? Failure, and a lot of it! His ability to succeed in what he does pales in comparison to his ability to fail. He has essentially paved his way to success with failures, and he's living proof that if you master the art of failure, it will never be something you're ashamed of again.

No matter what you do, no matter how much you plan ahead or how much brainpower you put into things, one fact remains: failure is a part of life, and it's definitely a part of success. Understanding this is vital to getting what you want and achieving any goal you set for yourself.

That's why today, I want to take a look at all of Elon Musk's most important failures so we can understand what he's done with it and learn by example.

No One Would Hire Him As CEO

A 24-year-old Elon Musk and his brother Kimbal Musk founded their first company in 1995, known as Zip2. This company found success by providing customizable city guides to the Bay Area newspapers so they could adapt to the online world.

At this time, Elon Musk was driven, committed, and combative. Even back then, he and his brother would go to great lengths to save money and give their all to the company. He hadn't learned about failure just yet. He used to think he would rather die than fail; that philosophy would change.

When investors started to note Zip2, they didn't want this version of Elon Musk as CEO. He was the chief technology officer instead, and he had no control of the vision of a company he created. When the company went through an expensive and botched merger, Musk demanded to be CEO, but it didn't happen. He was actually further isolated from power.

The Elon Musk of the 1990s was the kind of leader who would rewrite the work of his engineering team because he believed they were incompetent and who would publicly shame employees for their mistakes, without knowing, this would directly affect their productiveness. He wasn't a good manager, he failed at that, but he learned that management meant working with people, not against them.

Zip2 went on to be bought by Compaq in 1999 for $307 million, of which Musk received $22 million. Enough money to start a new venture, which would lead him to all the revolutionary businesses we know today.

But money wasn't the most important thing he got out of this experience; it was the realization that he failed to earn a position as the head of his own company and that it was as bad an idea as everyone else believed. Coming to terms with this fact would serve him well in the long-run, and it was the first of many failures that would enable him to become who he is today.

Near Bankruptcy & SpaceX

SpaceX had a rocky start, to say the least. In fact, Elon Musk almost lost everything when the third space rocket the company produced exploded at launch. A few other explosions after that made him lose Facebook and NASA satellites, so he took a series of important hits.

This is a decade after Zip2, and the value of failure has cemented in his brain by now. He speaks of SpaceX's initial failure by saying: "There's a silly notion that failure's not an option at NASA, but it is. If things are not failing, it means you're not innovating enough." That's a long way from the guy who claimed he would rather commit Seppuku (Japanese ritual suicide) than fail.

If we look at Elon Musk's career, one of the take-aways is that the path towards success involves a lot of failures. And the SpaceX failure is something he's still learning from. SpaceX rockets have become more reliable than they've ever been, and all launches have been successful this year. That's a long way from almost going bankrupt.

SpaceX started with just a few people who didn't know much about making rockets, and Elon Musk became chief engineer and designer not because he wanted to, but because no one good would join his team. This led to many exploding rockets and nearly running out of money. His first three launches failed, and he could've called it quits, take what was left of the money and give up. But he didn't, he built another rocket with the money that was left, and that fourth one worked. If it had failed, it would've been the end of SpaceX.

If Elon Musk still thought about failure the way he did in 1995, humanity wouldn't be looking at the possibility of colonizing Mars and further space travel. Let that sink in for a minute.

Near Bankruptcy & Tesla

SpaceX wasn't the only company to almost go under. Tesla was also weeks away from ceasing to exist because it was bleeding money nonstop. This was due to the Model 3 production ramp, but Elon Musk put all his efforts into pulling Tesla back from the edge of oblivion.

He worked even more than he already does, and he claims his seven-day workweeks pained him, and he doesn't recommend this to anyone. But if he didn't, the company wouldn't still be here today.

The marketing concerns surrounding Model 3 are a public secret, and even though the pre-order level showed success, the same couldn't be said of the production level. The challenge here was to produce enough electric vehicles to meet the demand, and they just couldn't do it. Luckily, Elon Musk had the determination and stamina necessary to act fast and solve the problems that were threatening death in a short period of time, but it was difficult, and it surely came at a cost. Not just for Elon Musk, who practically lived on the production site, but also for employees who had to work long hours.

Tesla's dark period ran between March and April of 2018, so the blow is quite recent. This period officially came to an end when the company was able to hit the production target of 5000 vehicles per week in July 2018. Only four months later! Think about how incredible that is; facing one of the biggest failures an entrepreneur can face and saying, "no, that's not how it's going to go."

When Tesla finally met the production target, Elon Musk asked his employees to go a step further and reach the mark of 6000 cars per week. This is what allowed the company to turn a profit for the first time in two years, and it's the reason Tesla is still alive today, innovating and right at the forefront of the industry.

Struggle to Mass Produce Electric Cars

The subject of Tesla's near-bankruptcy brings us to another big failure, which is the struggle to mass-produce electric cars, a problem that has been present quite a bit in Elon Musk's career in the automobile industry.

Elon Musk has revolutionized the manufacturing process because meeting Tesla's demand is one of the biggest challenges he's had to face. Model S attracts orders without a problem, but the issue is that factory capacity and mass-production are important hurdles for the company.

One of the moves made to further this objective was to shut down the factory in Fremont, California, to improve the assembly line operation. However, it's difficult to make sure that all the pieces of factory equipment work as they should, so it delayed the plan to reach their production numbers, which were projected at 35,000. In the end, they produced 2,000 fewer cars than expected, and that was a big hit for the company.

Elon Musk talked about upgrading the factory, and he claims it is like "changing the wheels on a bus while going down the freeway." His perfectionist attitude has also become an issue, and he has been faced with the possibility that being so perfectionist with his products truly affects production and it does more harm than good in the long run.

Tesla executives have had to learn to manage suppliers, design and operate factory equipment, troubleshoot problems quickly, and implement good quality control. All of these are key elements of the manufacturing process, which is by no means an easy and simple task. You don't know how hard it is to produce something until you're doing it, and with vehicles, that's even more challenging, especially innovative vehicles. A complicated car such as Model S, for example, requires 70,000 unique parts. Try to wrap your brain around that for a minute.

Imagine what it takes to build an even more complicated and innovative car such as Model X. Model X was revealed in 2015, and the first ones began shipping later that same year. But the troubles soon began, and Tesla was unable once more to deliver the numbers because there were nowhere near enough supplier parts. Another big issue was the fact that the first version of Model X simply had too much new technology, and it was difficult to keep up. See what Elon Musk means about perfectionism being a problem?

Perhaps that's exactly the core of the issue with Tesla production. It's one thing to have the desire to put your vision on the market exactly as you've conceived it, and it's another thing altogether to bring that vision to reality, especially when we're talking about something you need to produce in big numbers.

This, of course, won't stop Elon Musk from bringing his vision forwards. He understands that failure is not the end of the line. In fact, something better often comes after failure because it teaches you valuable lessons; it gives you the knowledge you need to adjust and to push forward.

He has done it many times before, and he will do it many times more because failure has become a part of who he is as an entrepreneur and as a person. And it's his attitude towards failure, his commitment to his ideas, what allows him to create such wonderful things and to enjoy so much success.

Final Words

Elon Musk has more than done well for himself. Genius CEO of SpaceX, Tesla, the Boring Company, and many other successful projects at the forefront of major industries, has managed to realize some of the most incredible ambitions a person has ever had.

But how is that possible? How has he managed to improve not just his life but that of humanity as a whole? What is the secret of his success? Well, the secret is to accept failure and to work with what it has to teach you.

By looking at Elon Musk's mistakes, it's easy to see that they've actually enabled him instead of holding him back. His companies have introduced solar power technology, they've made commercial spaceflight available, they've produced and sold amazing, futuristic electric cars, and they're working on things that will change our lives forever.

Elon Musk's Hair Transformation

If you haven't seen Elon Musk in his 20s, you might not be able to trace his transformation in terms of facial appearance. Despite being a famous entrepreneur, Elon Musk was just like any other man who faces hair loss at an early age. However, there is a secret to share with you: He has yielded a noticeable change in his looks by undergoing a hair treatment.

If you want to trace the radical shift in his style, you might have to go back to the mid-90s, when he was quickly losing hair at the front of his head. This hair loss soon spread across his head. During this time, Elon was seen with thin hair, especially above his ears, which certainly disclosed that he was doing something to stop this damage. Within a couple of years, he was seen with new, thick hair.

Elon never spoke publicly about the details of his hair transformation or the therapy he went through. However, as suggested from his pictures and videos, he might have tried either hair loss medication and/or a hair transplant. The first technique helps in stopping further hair loss instead of encouraging the growth of new follicles. However, looking at Elon Musk's makeover, the chances of his hair being restored by this technique are small. Apart from that, medication has side effects, like skin rashes, swelling, and sometimes impotence. Plus, Elon would have been required to take medicines for a longer time. Considering all these factors, it is likely that this renowned businessman chose a hair transplant method, which is technically advanced and produces better results in appearance than the old-style hair plugs. A few other positive points Elon Musk might have found in this technique are the shorter length of time required by the surgical procedures, the easy transfer of hair follicles, and the transplanting of real hair from one section of the scalp to the other. Additionally, he fulfilled all the criteria required for a hair transplant: a stable and sufficient supply of donor's hair so that it could be used to cover the bald zone and for use in future hair transplants.

If you observe the position Elon Musk held in terms of global businesses and technological advancements, it is obvious that he did not require a facelift. However, with his transformed look achieved via a hair transplant, he has certainly brought his best image into existence.

Section 5
Tesla Fud and Mars Colonization

CHAPTER ONE

ELON MUSK VERSUS SHORTS: HOW FUD AFFECTS TESLA MARKET VALUE—AND WHY IT MATTERS?

Introduction

If you've never heard about short selling stock, you're not alone. In fact, before Tesla CEO Elon Musk engaged in a highly publicized war with short sellers, many were content to simply let the practice fly under the radar.

With Musk coming out strong against short sellers and Tesla fear-mongering over the last couple of years—and with high-notoriety SEC lawsuits against Musk making the headlines—it's important that aspiring investors, entrepreneurs, and Elon Musk fans alike understand the current situation.

In this chapter, we'll look at the practice of short selling and how it relates to Elon Musk and Tesla in particular. In addition, we'll take a closer look at Musk's response to short selling practices and examine the fairness of SEC responses regarding Musk's behavior.

With the issue of short selling and the dispersion of negative press and FUD (fear, uncertainty, and doubt) that potentially plagued Tesla and Musk in 2018, 2019, and 2020, understanding what the relevant concepts are can help us to predict Tesla's path forward and anticipate the company's direction leading into the future.

For this reason, let's take a look at these issues, starting with the practice of short selling itself.

What is Short Selling?

Let's start with an important question: what is short selling? While the practice itself is quite old in trade, it's not one that most amateur investors are familiar with. In fact, before Musk brought the issue to light, it was hardly publicized at all.

In order to best understand the concept, we must first look at traditional investment. In traditional stock trading, the goal is to buy low and to sell high. This means that you try to buy stocks that are currently priced low, banking on the supposition that you will be able to trade them for a higher value and thus make more money.

Short selling, on the other hand, works as the exact opposite. When an investor short sells, he borrows stocks at a higher value and sells them immediately. The goal is to find a company that one believes will end up decreasing in value. Once that happens, the investor can buy the stocks back again for a lower price and essentially pocket the difference.

For the sake of example, let's say that you borrow twenty shares of Tesla stock for two hundred dollars apiece. This means that you borrow a total of four thousand dollars' worth of Tesla stock. The short seller, believing that the stock would devalue, would turn around and immediately sell the stock, wait for it to devalue, and buy it back up. If the stock devalued to only one hundred dollars a share, when the short seller returns the shares to the lending company, he would have pocketed two thousand dollars (minus a small borrowing cost).

As you might imagine, short selling is quite the gamble. Specifically, there's never any guarantee that a company will decrease in stock value, even if market trends seem to suggest so. In reality, companies can end up riding a wave that increases their value and puts short sellers at an extreme loss. What's more, unlike traditional modes of investment, short-sellers aren't capped off at losing simply one hundred percent of their investments.

This means that short-sellers could end up losing much more than what they initially gambled. For this reason, many short sellers engage in practices that could make the value of a company's stock go down. Still, with so much on the line, any short sell is a risky investment.

This begs the question: if the practice is so much of a gamble, why short sell at all?

Why Short Sell?

Would you make an investment if you knew that you were at risk of posting a five hundred percent loss? While all conventional logic points to no, the reality is that many short sellers engage in such risky practices every day. This leads many to question why short selling is such a common practice, to begin with. After all, the practice seems to take the already risky venture of stock investment and trading and place it on steroids.

Despite this, there are a variety of reasons why short-sellers decide to engage in the practice. For starters, for those who are able to do it well, short selling can lead to massive economic rewards. If one is able to capitalize on companies that are trending downward—especially large firms like Tesla, Apple, or Amazon—they will be able to pocket quite a bit of change.

Additionally, many find that short selling is easier than it appears on the surface. By spreading FUD, many short sellers are able to create uncertainty about a particular company, meaning they can devalue the stock and secure their investment.

If you're like Musk, you may have read that last statement and thought, "Wait, is that even legal?" While spreading fear, uncertainty, and doubt to lower the stock and trade value of a company may sound like something that would raise alarm bells with the SEC, the truth of the matter is that there's nothing illegal about short selling as long as it's done within boundaries.

What are those boundaries? It's simple enough. In short, a short seller is able to spread negativity as long as that negativity appears to be grounded in reality. Take, for example, Tesla. When the company failed to meet its Q4 goals in 2018, short sellers were able to use this negative fact as speculation that the company was in a downward spiral.

Of course, this only hurts Tesla's trade value. Still, many would argue that the short-sellers have done nothing wrong. As spreading speculation about a company is legal so long as the short seller is not spewing libel or making up false claims, short-sellers are vindicated in the practice of downplaying a company's economic future in order to decrease company value.

That's why Musk has called short sellers "value destroyers." The tech entrepreneur has further challenged these short sellers to bet against his multi-billion-dollar car company Tesla, which has repeatedly proved investors wrong by forging a new path for the electric motor industry.

In light of this, it becomes useful to view Musk's own history with short sellers to see why the genius entrepreneur is vindicated in wishing for the practice of short selling to be criminalized. As part of this, we'll also take a look at some of Musk's own responses to short selling devaluation—many of which have been called into question by detractors and even by the SEC.

How Has Short Selling Affected Tesla?

With all this in mind, how has short-selling affected Tesla—and what exactly has made Musk so angry? Over the last several years, Tesla has frequently been one of the top targets in the nation for short selling. In fact, as recently as April 2018, the electric car company was the largest victim of short sells, with twenty-five percent of its shares falling in the short sell market.

No wonder, then, that CEO Elon Musk had begun to grow outraged. The tech genius is not only competing with others in the market but also with short sellers who attempt to devalue his company and produce worse results. In an increasingly competitive age, the practice of short selling looks to do significant damage.

In 2018 alone, Tesla's share price decreased 2.2 percent, despite Musk's insistence that the company is now closer than ever to developing a fully-functional, affordable electric vehicle. Much of this decline was a result of short-sellers, who were able to capitalize off rising Tesla losses.

In 2019, Tesla reclaimed the spot as the number one shorted company in the United States, a position that had been held by Apple since 2016. But why has Tesla emerged as such a strong target for short selling? Better yet, what is it that makes the company sustainable to such high levels of speculation?

According to Goldman Sachs, much of it has to do with investors' belief that Tesla won't be able to fulfill its production goals. In an interview, one analyst remarked, "We believe the sustainable production rate for the second quarter of 2018 is most likely below the 2,000 vehicles mark the company achieved in the final week of the [first] quarter."

In other words, investors aren't buying into what they see as inflated production goals set by the company. This speculation by one of the top stock firms in the United States has made it trendy for investors to turn against Musk and Tesla. Known for setting lofty goals in what is largely an unproven niche, the company was already a prime target for short selling. Combined with the serial entrepreneur's tendency to set high goals and oversell his products, it's no wonder that Tesla has held onto its spot as the number one short-sold company in the United States.

But how exactly has this short-selling helped to devalue Tesla? Let's take a look.

Short Selling and FUD

As executives across the country admit, the true danger in short selling comes not from potential losses—which occur only in a tiny minority of cases—but in the ability of the short sellers to generate negative press about a particular company. In reality, it depends on the ability of the general public—and the media—to pick up on this press if the actual short selling will inflict any damage.

In other words, it can be said that the success of the short seller largely relies on their ability to generate fear, uncertainty, and doubt regarding a specific company. By playing on market fears, these sellers are able to sap a company of its attractiveness and cast doubt on its future success.

Unfortunately, as it relates to Tesla, short-sellers have been able to dominate the media narrative. As Peter Forman of CleanTechnica explains, the media are more than willing to latch onto FUD Tesla narratives, painting a bleak picture of the company's prospects to others in the market. He explains, "When an analyst who is bullish on Tesla appears on a business news channel such as CNBC, that analyst is grilled by the hosts with the short seller themes du jour in a manner that assumes the shorts are right."

In other words, anti-Tesla stances have become the default in the mainstream media, driving Tesla stocks to devaluation and short-sellers to an all-time high in Tesla market capitalization. Indeed, Forman credits a 2018 *New York Times* interview as facilitating a Tesla stock price drop in excess of $30 a share. This drop, which occurred the day after Musk's maligned interview with the newspaper, saw a transfer of over one billion dollars' worth of wealth from Tesla investors to the pockets of short-sellers.

According to some Musk supporters, this represents one of the greatest recent successes of the anti-Musk short-seller crowd.

This raises the question: why has the media been so ready to latch onto negative press as it pertains to Tesla? Over the last decade, the electric car company has nearly singlehandedly been able to revive the electric automobile market and has produced the bestselling line of electric vehicles ever made. In doing so, the company has also made electric cars more affordable for consumers across the globe.

All of this has been part of Musk's larger vision to help revolutionize transportation and change the world. The last several years have seen Musk develop a cult of personality enamored with his ideas and his visions for making the world a safer and more convenient place. Musk, who has publicly stated the desire to positively influence the world through transportation reform and a move away from fossil fuels, is also one of the leading producers and innovators of solar energy in the United States.

With all these intentions being good, it's worth asking why the media has taken blatantly negative stances when it comes to Tesla's chances in the market. The truth of the matter is that short-sellers have been able to capitalize on the volatility of the electric car industry, as well as some of Musk's own comments to develop plausible narratives that have caused investors—and analysts—to shy away from outright support of the brand.

In other words, short-sellers have taught the market to approach Tesla with caution. This, combined with Musk's hostility against short sellers, tendency to oversell and exaggerate his numbers and goals, and legal troubles with the SEC, have facilitated an environment where the support of Tesla appears not only foolish but dangerous.

For this reason, it becomes crucial to take a look at Musk's response to short-sellers to see how the tech genius is handling the FUD press and examine the reasons why Tesla continues to succeed despite being the largest victim of short selling in the United States.

Musk's Response to Short Sellers

Before we can answer any of those questions, it's imperative to first take a look at Musk's personal responses to the practice of short selling. Those who are aware of the current war between Musk, the press and short-sellers may be surprised to learn that the tech entrepreneur, who has recently suggested that short selling should invoke criminal penalties, has not always been against the practice.

In a 2012 statement, the CEO and product architect of Tesla, Inc. was quoted as saying that while "[short sellers] cause me grief; I would defend the rights of shorts to exist." In the statement, Musk, like many others, was perhaps referring to the idea that shorts provide a valuable first line of defense against market abuse by major firms.

The idea behind this is simple: that shorts point out some of the biggest flaws in a company—flaws that might otherwise be pushed under the radar for large firms that are able to lobby for better press coverage and for an enhanced brand image. Musk, who at the time had only been CEO of the burgeoning Tesla company for four years, would quickly change his tune regarding short selling.

Just a few years later, the tech genius was quoted as saying, "The last several years have taught me that [short sellers] are reasonably maligned. What they do should be illegal." Musk's comments come on the heels of aggressive FUD campaigning that spun a negative narrative regarding his Tesla brand. Namely, media portrayals of Tesla as a company on its last legs—which seem to appear every quarter—helped devalue Tesla stock and keep the company well below its trading goals.

Over the last seven years, short selling has cost Tesla billions of dollars in potential value and has generated popular sentiment away from the brand. In fact, it could be said that the FUD campaigns that have been put out to smear Tesla's image have indeed had long-term impacts on brand success. By painting Tesla as a company with a bleak economic future in an already volatile electric cars market, FUD-propagating short sellers have been able to limit popular acceptance of electric vehicles, which, while still growing, perhaps has been kept short of its potential.

This means that Tesla and Musk have potentially lost out on billions in long-term value due to unearned market speculation that has largely proven to be false. However, despite Tesla's ability to consistently prove detractors wrong, the company has remained a top target for short selling.

And Musk is fighting it every step of the way. In a recent tweet, the tech genius encouraged shorts to "place their bets" after Goldman Sachs indicated that they were cutting Tesla's price targets. The tweet was interpreted as a challenge to shorts who would run with the FUD press in an attempt to devalue Tesla currency.

While Musk's fans enjoy the genius's engagement with shorts and other adversaries on Twitter, outsiders see the Tesla CEO's tweets as just another reason the company has fallen victim to large amounts of FUD press. In fact, even many Musk supporters have suggested that the serial entrepreneur's tweeting habits may be more trouble than they are worth.

Over the last year alone, Elon has had three major run-ins with the SEC and other plaintiffs who allege that Musk is using Twitter as a platform to inflate company figures, mislead investors, and damage shareholders. The trend started in August 2018, when the SEC filed a lawsuit against Musk for tweeting out that he planned on taking the company private. The tweet, which shocked investors around the world, was eventually backtracked, leading some to suspect that Musk merely did so to throw off shorts and other detractors who constantly attempted to devalue the company.

These fears proved to be right, as emails leaked from early August revealed that Musk had sent an email to Tesla's board of directors with the following subject line: "Offer to Take Tesla Private at $420." The body of the message criticized "constant defamatory attacks by the short-selling community, resulting in great harm to our valuable brand."

Despite the email, the Tesla board of directors were shocked at Musk's tweet—as were Tesla shareholders, one of whom texted, "What's Elon's tweet about? Can't make any sense of it."

The confusion and fallout of the tweet led the SEC to file a lawsuit against Musk, who eventually settled the suit by stepping down from his chair on the board of directors and agreeing to pay a twenty million dollar fine.

Not to be deterred; however, the tech genius continued his Twitter antics, tweeting in February 2019 that his Tesla brand would produce 500,000 cars in 2019. The numbers, which were largely viewed as inflated and meant to drive up the company's value, were subject to much criticism, leading the SEC to ask a court to hold the serial entrepreneur in contempt.

Following this, law firm Grant & Eisenhofer sued Elon Musk on behalf of investors, citing the genius entrepreneur's actions as dangerous to the market and to individual investors alike. In a statement, Grant & Eisenhofer Director Michael Barry remarked, "He has ignored federal court orders, a settlement with the SEC, and his company's own corporate policies expressly requiring that any of his tweets regarding Tesla be pre-screened. His conduct has not only cost shareholders dearly but threatens to expose the company to even greater liability and litigation in the future."

Barry's sentiment was one that was picked up by the mainstream media, which criticized the serial entrepreneur's actions and used them to further fuel the FUD short-selling market. To the delight of shorts, the media portrayal of Musk has become one of an irresponsible celebrity genius who doesn't mind recklessly endangering his brand—and shareholders—in order to prove a point.

The fallout of Musk's actions has led to three distinct camps: those who side with the engineering genius and enjoy his tactics that point out the unfairness of the system, others who support Tesla but not the way Musk is handling the situation and those who side with the short sellers and believe that they are doing important work.

Those in the second camp point to the fact that Tesla's short stocks were driven up to $800 million the day Musk arrived in court in early April 2019. These individuals claim that, ironically, Musk's attempt at shorting the shorts led only to an increase in the amount of short selling of Tesla stock. This phenomenon was only boosted by the fact that Tesla's production numbers fell far short of their lofty predictions. Pro-Musk crowds point to the fact that Tesla has remained the number one electric automobile manufacturer in the world and emphasize the impact of Musk's brand image on continued Tesla success. As part of this, these individuals point out that one of the central reasons fans are so enamored with Musk is because of his ability to challenge his adversaries head-on.

In regard to the situation, short-sellers wholeheartedly defend their right to devalue the brand. One short-seller writes, "Elon's cult of personality has attracted thousands of people who simply cannot believe he could ever fail or be wrong. These are the same people who get harmed when Elon tweets fake buyout offers, goes on Twitter rampages late at night, etc. We shorts really just want to see to this farce, one way or another."

In other words, shorts believe that they are saving shareholders and consumers from potential damage that could advertently or inadvertently come from Musk. While the notion that Musk is out to harm his shareholders is ludicrous, many in the pro-Musk crowd agree that the serial entrepreneur tows a fine line when it comes to his Twitter usage and product overselling.

This leads us to a central question: is Musk in the right? Let's examine the situation in detail.

Is Musk Right?

Elon Musk has called for the criminalization of short selling, even as his detractors point out that his Twitter antics aren't much better. Still, fans point to the fact that Musk—who is simply trying to maintain his brand's value and protect his assets from malign damage—has done no wrong. These individuals insist instead that Musk is in the right and that if anyone should be fined by the SEC, it should be the shorts who purposely sell out Tesla value in order to make a quick buck.

This begs the central question of whether or not Musk is justified in his approach against the shorts. In order to answer this question, it's important to analyze why Musk resorts to such actions in the first place. The tech CEO watches as billions of dollars are wiped from his company's value on an annual basis—and can do nothing about it.

And while a case could be made that shorts exist in order to keep sellers honest and protect consumers from malign trade practices, the truth of the matter is that shorts help propagate a FUD machine that can spell disaster for companies and their value. In fact, according to speculation from Musk fans, it is this short selling, fueled in part by actions on the part of entities such as the SEC, that has backed Musk into a corner.

While speculation, this is worth noting, as the case can be made that what has truly put Tesla behind over the past year is not Musk's Twitter behavior but the seemingly arbitrary way in which the SEC enforces its standards. In other words, while it's deemed okay for shorts to deliberately devalue a company, it's not okay for the CEO of that company to fight back and try and retain its value.

This double standard rests at the core of Musk's dissatisfaction and the growing unease among his fans. Though Musk has agreed to tone down his Twitter usage—a move that has many breathing sighs of relief—the fact is that the matter still remains. At the end of the day, Musk and Tesla are still left at the mercy of shorts who will stop at nothing to devalue the company to make a pretty big buck.

So, what can Musk do? Considering that fighting fire with fire will only land the serial entrepreneur in trouble with the SEC and others in court, what is the best route possible left for Musk? Unfortunately, the serial entrepreneur has only one "legal" weapon at his disposal: his success.

With a stronger and more successful Tesla, Musk will be able to prove the negative press wrong and upgrade the value of his stock. Luckily for Musk, the serial entrepreneur has shown time and again that he can do just that. Now, as critics doubt that he will be able to pull off a fully-functional and affordable electric vehicle, Musk has the opportunity to up the value of Tesla's stock by releasing a vehicle that defies expectations.

According to the serial entrepreneur, the company's recently released Model 3 will do just that. The first Tesla car is meant for the average consumer; the product retails for around $35,000. If Musk can pull off the success of the Model 3 long term, he'll be able to reverse the damage short sellers have inflicted on the company over the past year and lead Tesla into a new era. The feat, however, looks to be a big one, as many critics doubt that the company will be able to sell such sophisticated technology for a low price and still maintain a healthy profit margin.

Ultimately, the answer to whether or not Musk's unorthodox business practices are right will ultimately be played out in the success of Tesla in the years to come. If Musk can continue his cult of personality and use his increased brand image to leverage more Tesla sales, it's likely that his Twitter antics and often-times wild commentary can pay off. Specifically, if Musk's increasing popularity can be used to raise Tesla's brand strength and offset the damage of his several high-profile lawsuits, it can be said that the genius's tweets did more good than harm.

How Should We View Musk?

With all this being said, what should we believe about the eccentric Tesla CEO? Opinions on the serial entrepreneur's antics are as varied as the colors of the rainbow. A close look at Musk's supporters reveal that many view his strategies as an attempt to defend their investments. More specifically, small investors who have put their savings into Tesla stock see Musk's actions as a way of securing their investment and keeping them from going under.

In this way, Musk has emerged as a champion of small investors across the industry, who by nature are routinely hurt the most from short sellers. With Musk's calls for the abolition of short selling, small investors around the nation are gaining hope that they'll gain another layer of protection when it comes to their assets.

This represents yet another way that Musk, who has remained committed over the last two decades to revolutionizing the world and making the planet healthier and more sustainable for future generations, is helping the average man. By ending the short-selling practice, Musk would be able to free smaller investors from the fear of losing their investments to the whims of FUD-sharing short-sellers,

In short, the situation can be viewed in the following light: Musk is at war not only with short-sellers but with the ill-intentioned fear, uncertainty, and doubt that these sellers continuously promulgate. At its core, this is a war not just between Musk and short sellers, but between value and devaluation—and ultimately, what it means for the consumer.

For this reason, it's crucial that we take a moment to see why the average consumer should take Musk's side when it comes to the short-selling issue.

How We Should Respond

As consumers, there's only one clear way that we should respond to the current war between Musk and his Tesla short-sellers, and that is to back the serial entrepreneur wholeheartedly. Yes, that's even if we don't fully agree with Musk's unconventional Twitter strategies.

Here's why: the battle between Musk and short sellers will ultimately decide the fate of the consumer. Though those who support the short-selling practice emphasize its role in protecting the consumer, the reality could not be further from the truth. Outside of theoretical bounds, shorts exist only to malign the customer by reducing the amount of value that can be extracted from companies.

Tesla is a prime example. Under Musk's leadership, the company has grown into the most successful electric automobile enterprise to ever exist. In the process, Musk has helped millions switch over to electric cars, reducing the carbon footprint and placing a stronger emphasis on cleaner energy.

For the consumer, this means that strengthening the Tesla brand should be a top priority. Without the company, the world is left with a litany of fossil-fuel-guzzling automobile manufacturers who don't give the same consideration to environmental issues. What's more, if Tesla didn't exist today, the world would lose one of the leading promulgators of solar energy.

This means that the value of the Tesla brand extends far beyond Musk's current accomplishments. With tons of potential value that could revolutionize humankind, the company is a treasure among current organizations. This means that any attempt to reduce the value of the company and cause it to falter should be taken as an affront to the success of humanity.

And, really, that's what the war is all about. This means that the fight isn't between Musk and the SEC or even Musk and his short sellers. It's about the right of the consumer to maintain access to a brighter future. For this reason, it's crucial that consumers realize the importance of siding with Musk as it relates to their own wellbeing.

The battle between Musk and dangerous short-sellers only looks to intensify as Tesla heads into a crucial year that has already seen the unveiling of the company's much-anticipated Model Y. With many analysts seeing the year as a "make or break" year for the company's image heading into the future, it's crucial that consumers become more aware of the battle between Musk and his shorts and do their part to keep the Tesla brand strong and alive.

Short Burn Of The Century

On May 4, 2018, Elon Musk tweeted that a short burn of the century was coming soon. When he tweeted this, many people were skeptical because they knew that this wasn't possible. However, twenty-four months later, Musk made good on this tweet.

Tesla Inc.'s car deliveries and quarterly profits increased significantly in late 2019 and for all of 2020. This led to a sustained and significant increase in the share price of the company throughout 2020 to a high that nobody could have imagined in 2018. Tesla's share price increased over 700% in 2020 alone, and Tesla's short-sellers endured at least $35 billion in losses in 2020. This was because the rapidly increasing share price forced the short-sellers to cover their positions by purchasing Tesla shares at very high prices (short squeeze). Musk and his supporters described it as the "short burn of the century." Of course, it took longer than anticipated after Musk tweeted, but eventually, he did make good on his promise.

After so many short-sellers profited from the dips in the stock price of Tesla, the increased vehicle production and sales finally gave them the lesson that Musk wanted them to learn.

Why Did Tesla Launch Short Shorts for Real?

What began as a joke by Elon Musk is now happening for real. Yes, Tesla has extended its product range to include a pair of shorts that are available for purchase online. People on the internet and Musk's fans are giving tremendous responses to this product. Tesla's website is flooded with orders to buy these world-famous shorts.

As we know, the stock price for the renowned electric automobile company is reaching new heights in recent months. This was obvious after it announced a better performance in the second- and third-quarter results in 2020. Tesla did much better in terms of quantity of delivery than expected.

Musk's opponents were losing all their money in the stock market as Tesla's share price reached $1200. Certainly, he did not lose this opportunity to mock them, through Twitter, via Tesla shorts. In technical terms, 'shorting' means selling off one's stock. Musk has taken a diplomatic view on this, as he refers to 'shorts' as people who are willing to go short on Tesla's share. This is basically a taunt of those who bet on the company's share price going low.

There was a time when Elon Musk made fun of these 'shorts' by saying that Tesla would create amazing short shorts in sparkling satin red with gold trim. Now his statement has become a reality, as Tesla has launched a pair of these shorts for online purchase. The shorts are available at 'shop.tesla.com,' where other vehicle accessories and Tesla apparel is also for sale.

Along with its color and texture, other significant features of the shorts include the Tesla logo on the front and the phrase 'S3XY' at the back. The description of the product includes a sarcastic comment: "enjoy the exceptional comfort from the closing bell."

Immediately after their launch, the internet fell in love with the shorts. In fact, people overloaded the website with exceptional traffic. The craziness of Tesla followers broke the shop website as soon as Elon Musk declared the link to this product on his Twitter handle. Seeing this, the crowd rushed to place their orders, which caused the website to malfunction. Within 30 minutes of this announcement, more than 30K engagements were spotted with this tweet.

The price of the shorts is yet another point of discussion, as $69.420 is a unique number in itself. The first part of it is derived from the adolescent witticism and the second part denotes the price at which Musk, a few years ago, wished to take Tesla private. This price seems to be inconsequential today, as the stock has hit a price more than eight times this value.

When TSLA was at $420, the SEC charged Musk against his 'secured funding' statement. So, Musk had plans to give them some Tesla shorts. David Einhorn, a well-known hedge fund manager who was strongly bearish on Tesla stock, also received a box of Tesla shorts from Elon Musk.

Long story short, the big-time joke about Tesla going short is no longer a joke. The company has converted it into an actual product that is available on the website for purchase.

CHAPTER TWO

ARE ELON MUSK'S PROJECTS ALL MEANT TO FURTHER HIS PLANS FOR MARS?

Elon Musk, as you already know, is one of the most popular entrepreneurs and engineers in the world. He's a workaholic, and he's quite literally at the forefront of everything that matters today.

Perhaps one of his most ambitious goals is the colonization of Mars. That's why today we want to take a look at all of Elon Musk's most important projects and see how they help him further his main cause: setting up a self-sustaining base on Mars we can turn to in the event something catastrophic happens here on Earth. But more on that later!

Here are some of Elon Musk's most relevant projects and what they mean for his Mars plan, in no particular order:

SpaceX

The Space Exploration Technologies Corporation, popularly known as SpaceX, is one of the biggest businesses founded by Elon Musk and also one of the most well-known modern manufacturers of space transportation systems there is.

Musk's initial concept for this company, which was published in 2001, focused on Mars landing and building an "oasis."

SpaceX's role in Elon Musk's ultimate mission to colonize Mars is quite obvious, and it's the company that stands right at the center of everything. But let's continue and see how other projects come into the mix.

Starlink

Starlink is another massive project, and it consists of a group of orbital communication satellites that should provide Internet access on a worldwide scale.

The commercial objectives of the project are obvious; after all, they will be distributing Internet connections all around the world. This means SpaceX will have a huge source of income and this goal also gives Starship-Super Heavy rockets another purpose.

When we look at this project with the Mars colonization in mind, Starlink will be a vital element of the communication infrastructure on the red planet. For Mars colonizers, it would be very difficult to construct all the complex networks, antennas, towers, etc., not to mention it would be dangerous and expensive. Starlink brings a part of this infrastructure to space, so it takes care of the problem of bringing it to Mars.

SolarCity & Tesla

In simple terms, SolarCity generates electricity, and Tesla uses it. On earth, solar energy is developing quickly, it's also more efficient and very popular, and electric cars are more effective, economical and they conquer the market.

On Mars, only electricity will be useful when it comes to transport because there's no oil (that we know of), and so by the time colonization is a fact, Tesla will have enough technology to create electric transport specifically for Mars. Electricity generation on Mars is not possible or practical with all the methods we have here on Earth, except one: solar energy. Elon Musk is a bit of an expert on solar energy at this point, so it's safe to say he'll know what to do on Mars when the time comes.

Transportation

Once Mars colonizers arrive on the red planet, they would have to start building residential areas, work areas, power plants, mining sites, and water and air production stations. All of this will be distributed throughout the planet, which means people will need a way to travel.

However, the solution is not as simple as building a Tesla bus specifically for Mars, but Elon Musk already knows what to do. The Boring Company is one of his proposals, which will create a network of underground tunnels under our cities so traffic can be redirected that way. There has been speculation of what the aim of The Boring Company actually is. Everyone speculates the digging of underground tunnels in LA has something to do with the Mars mission. Well, people may not be wrong.

Musk clarified in a conference that they would need to get good at digging if they plan on colonizing Mars. There is going to be a great deal of ice mining and mining in general as well to extract raw materials from Mars. They will have to utilize boring machines to find resources and mine ice on Mars.

On Earth, it's still to be seen if the concept of underground tunnels for transportation works or not, but on Mars, it may be perfect because the ecosystem of the planet is cruel. Mars has a weak magnetic field, and the planet is poorly protected from radiation, so the simplest solution is to go underground. The first colonies will most likely be built underground, so these underground tunnels will make it easy for people to access everything, and it will provide protection. Additionally, there's little to no seismic activity on Mars.

What will Mars colonizers use to move through these tunnels? Elon Musk's Hyperloop, of course! Hyperloop is Musk's take on a transportation system for passengers or freight where trains would move within tubes with reduced air pressure and the use of linear induction motors and air compressors as the source of acceleration. This would make the Hyperloop not only faster but more reliable and effective than any other source of transportation.

On Mars, the pressure on the surface and the density of air is so low that it presents an advantage to the Hyperloop.

Elon Musk's Plan to Colonize Mars

A lot has been said about Elon Musk's plan to colonize Mars, so I believe we should sum up all this information and get ourselves up to date with one of the most ambitious projects in history.

Starship (spacecraft) and (super heavy) rocket booster that are in development for the Mars missions are also meant to serve as point-to-point Earth transport and transport to the Moon and beyond. Elon Musk's goal is to phase out the Dragon, Falcon 9, and Falcon Heavy and rely instead on this new architecture for all future missions.

Testing is now underway, and if it is successful, the first Starship space flight could happen as soon as 2021, according to Musk. The first flights will be uncrewed and will only be for communication satellites. However, we know very little about the life-support system of the Starship.

If we compare these plans to the ones Elon Musk shared with the world at the International Astronautical Congress in Mexico and Adelaide, we can see a substantial evolution of his plans.

SpaceX's original plan was to take a million people to Mars in 40 to 100 years. This updated concept doesn't depart from that, but it gives us more insight into how Elon Musk plans to fund this new rocket and spacecraft, which is estimated to cost $10 billion. In short, Elon Musk already knows how to pay for it, and that's a huge step forwards and a piece of incredible news.

Elon Musk also spoke about how Mars colonists won't be living a glamorous life. He also addressed the misconception that surrounds his

Mars colonization project, which has people believing it will be meant as an escape plan for the rich.

Elon Musk's colonization vision is not about that at all. He stated, in fact, that the people who go to Mars will face far more dangers. It will be difficult, not at all glamorous, and there's a chance you'll die, but it's about more than danger; it's about exploration and literally reaching the next frontier.

If you want to understand what drives Elon Musk to focus so much energy and resources on this Mars colonization mission, then you must understand how he sees the future. His long-term objective with this mission is to provide a kind of plan B for society in case of an Extinction Level Event (ELE) such as nuclear destruction or an asteroid impact. He intends to put a million people on Mars so that there's enough seed of our civilization elsewhere for the human race to survive without reverting back to the dark ages.

Building a self-sustaining base on Mars is all about providing this option, and that's why he focuses mainly on Mars and not on the Moon because we're more likely to survive on the red planet than on a base at the Moon.

It's safe to say that Elon Musk takes the possibility of World War III very seriously, and it's his plan to settle this back-up civilization on Mars long before something like that happens. He doesn't believe we can avoid the possibility of another world war; to say it will never happen seems unlikely, and that's what fuels such an ambitious plan.

What we still don't know is how Elon Musk and SpaceX expect a Mars colony to survive for prolonged periods of time. It's still to be revealed how that can be made possible, and many of us have a million practical questions to ask.

What Elon Musk offers, though, is predictions on how he believes governance on Mars can look like in the future, which are also important to understand. For one, he imagines the Mars colony will operate under a direct democracy rather than the system of government we're accustomed to, which is a representative democracy. Musk expects this new society on Mars to vote directly on issues rather than having elected officials do it for them.

Elon Musk believes that representative democracy was the right system of government during the founding of our nation, where most people didn't know how to read or write. That won't be the case with a colony on Mars.

Musk also urged future colonists to keep laws short, so they can be easily understood and digested in order to vote for them. Long laws seem suspicious to him, and I believe we can all agree with that.

Another recommendation for future colonists is that the laws would be easier to repeal than to install in order to prevent arbitrary rules from restricting freedoms in the long run.

There's still a lot to be said about Elon Musk's plan for colonizing Mars, but the way things are going, I believe we'll have the answers to our questions sooner than we expect. Things have been moving at an incredible pace for this project, and it's not only exciting, it keeps us in awe of what one person's vision can do for the good of not just humanity but society as a whole.

Final Words

It's safe to say that everything Elon Musk is doing is meant to further his main mission and goal in life: colonizing Mars and providing a plan B so we can survive in the worst-case scenario. This means Elon Musk has a profound respect for humanity, and he's doing everything in his power to make sure that not only our lives are better right now, but also that we have a future no matter what happens. There's nothing more ambitious than that!

SECTION 6
HOW TO BE AS GREAT AS ELON MUSK?

CHAPTER ONE

POWER OF OPEN NETWORKS

When you think of Elon Musk, you probably think of traits such as motivation, self-drive, self-confidence, entrepreneurship, work ethic, perspective, and hard work, among many others.

When we are exposed to people like these, it's only natural to want to harvest the same traits and skills that make them so successful so we can apply them to our domain. That's why the question of how to be as great as Elon Musk is a question that has been thoroughly studied.

Entrepreneurs are especially interested in knowing the answer to this question, and the first thing we need to understand is that individual traits such as the ones mentioned above are not all it takes.

There are people out there who have an incredible work ethic and motivation, they come up with great ideas, and they make big plans for themselves, but they're still not at the same level of success as legends like Elon Musk, Steve Jobs, Bill Gates, Jeff Bezos, and others.

Being successful is about more than having the right values and traits, and it's definitely about a lot more than having intelligence. An overlooked aspect of success is that you need an open network to work with. In fact, according to many studies on the feel of network science, open networks are the best predictor for career success.

Why Are Open Networks So Important?

When you think of people like Elon Musk, two main things come to mind: his maniacal need for perfection and his insatiable curiosity. These are two traits that are often referred to as quirks, but they may have been the key determinant of his success.

When you work within a closed network, it means that you're only working with people who think alike, who never challenge your ideas or thoughts because they have the same viewpoint as you. This means that you're in an environment where your ideas and beliefs are constantly reaffirmed.

Working in an open network is the exact opposite because it means that you're constantly exposed to new ideas. People who work in this kind of network are significantly more successful. This is something the geniuses of our time have in common; their views are complex because they are constantly seeking out the new.

They don't limit themselves to their own ideas, their own skills. On the contrary, they're constantly exposing themselves to new perspectives, new fields, and they surround themselves with people who deeply understand different topics of interest.

What does this mean? This means that the structure of your network has a direct effect on how successful you can become. This might be news to some of you, and it's undoubtedly a concept that will require you to let go of a few beliefs before you can accept it, but it will change your perspective of success for the better.

After all, we need to be able to look at the complete picture if we want to harvest the success we desire for ourselves and our careers.

The Impact of Closed Networks

If we want to understand why open networks are so powerful, then it's important we understand why closed networks are not.

Closed networks are very common, and most people spend their careers in environments like that, full of people who already know each other. They are comfortable because there's a complete understanding of all the inner workings and unspoken rules and because the group has the same core beliefs. This means in a closed network, you share the way you see the world, and you're constantly reaffirming each other.

To understand why this is so, it's important to be aware of the fact that we've evolved to have an inner circle. This process of selection, so to speak, is how we determine whether we care about others or not. In short, we have an inner circle of people we trust, and strangers outside of it are not to be trusted.

This is the kind of behavior that has made it historically impossible for opposites to be able to work in conjunction. This is why religions have gone to war, why Democrats and Republicans are unable to agree on bills, why fads and social bubbles exist.

In short, by understanding why we behave this way, we can start making better sense of society as it is.

The Power of Open Networks

Open networks, as opposed to closed ones, pose unique opportunities and challenges to the people involved. Because these people are constantly converging with other groups, they foster unique relationships, they have exciting, unique experiences, and therefore their knowledge is broader, more varied, and even more profound than that of people in closed networks.

The challenge of approaching life this way is that it can lead to feeling like an outsider, and you will undoubtedly encounter people in life that will misunderstand and under-appreciate you simply because they don't understand the way your mind works.

But the most challenging part of all is that being a part of an open network and learning this way will require you to assimilate and integrate different perspectives and condense them into a single point of view that will rule the way you behave and the decisions you make.

This, as you can imagine, takes introspection, it takes energy, and it requires an unusually open mind that allows ideas to flow in and out. Once you're exposed to a new worldview, a new belief, or a new value, there's no going back. We all have experiences others won't be able to understand, and for this, we can feel like outsiders every time we come in contact with a new group of people.

This is by no means a huge obstacle, but you will have to learn how to deal with it. On the other hand, open networks offer a great array of opportunities.

For one, you gain a more accurate view of the world. When you immerse yourself in different groups and learn to see things from different perspectives, you harvest the skill of extracting useful information and preventing common mistakes because you have more than just one tool in your toolbox.

Additionally, you learn how to find the perfect timing for sharing information. You can learn something from one group and not be the first person to receive that information, but you can be the first person to introduce that knowledge into a different group. In short, you leverage the information you share to get a greater advantage.

When you can move from group to group, you become a sort of connector between them. In your role as an intermediary, you can create a great amount of value by connecting people or organizations that can edify each other, but that wouldn't be able to find each other on their own.

These are only a few of the many benefits of being able to coexist with many different people and harvest different beliefs and viewpoints.

How Open Networks Boost Creativity

What is creativity but the ability to connect things? The genius of people like Elon Musk is that they were able to find connections that no one else thought of before. How would that be possible if they stuck to immersing themselves in a single worldview? It couldn't be!

That's what's most beneficial about open networks, the fact that they allow us to access an incredible amount of information, they allow us to experience more than we ever thought possible, and as a result, we have more information than the average person.

When we have that, finding connections and creative ways of making things work becomes a higher possibility than ever. Creativity is the ability to synthesize all our knowledge and experience to create new things, and the reason people like Steve Jobs and Elon Musk could accomplish what they did, is that they had more experiences than other people, they had more knowledge, and they were more consistent with their thoughts because they had a goal.

Think of it this way: each new experience is another dot you can connect. If you don't seek that out, you're stuck in a linear understanding of the world and the way things work, which means you will only be able to move in one direction. The broader our human experience, the better we will be able to design our careers and our lives.

The Importance of Being Insatiable

One of the big differences between people like Elon Musk and the rest of the world is that they never stop being hungry for more. More knowledge, more experience. Their curiosity has been unparalleled, and their drive to understand more and more knows no bounds.

These are people that don't claim to know everything about anything. In fact, they're aware that there are many things they don't know yet, but they're never discouraged from seeking that knowledge and staying hungry.

There's no such thing as reaching a ceiling when it comes to knowledge or success because there's always something new to discover, something new to try, a new connection to see. Our experiences are infinite as long as we are alive, and understanding that, plus having the drive never to stop, is a big part of what makes these people so successful and unique.

We can all become the kind of person who achieves great things; what we have to do is start behaving in a way that makes such accomplishments possible.

CHAPTER TWO

HOW TO BE AS GREAT AS ELON MUSK?

Introduction

Elon Musk hasn't become one of the successful men of the twenty-first century by accident. The serial entrepreneur, who is responsible for such massive corporations as Tesla and SpaceX, has proven time and again that he belongs to an elite class of individuals, amassing a fortune that totals over ninety-four billion dollars as of 2019.

Of course, the genius entrepreneur and visionary didn't get this far without his share of positive attributes. People look to the tech giant, who strives to create a brighter, sustainable, and safer world for humankind, as a role model. As Musk's notoriety and success only grow, more individuals fall into his allure, all of this begging the question, "What can we do to become more like Elon Musk?"

In this chapter, we'll go over some of the entrepreneur's most defining characteristics and see what role they've played in his monumental success. Through this, we hope to establish a blueprint that others can use to model their lives after Musk and grow their personal and professional successes.

With this in mind, let's jump in and take a look at twenty-eight personality traits that individuals must harvest in order to be as great as Elon Musk!

Traits

By developing the following personality traits, you'll be one step closer to achieving Musk's success. For this reason, make sure you pay attention to the following tips so that you can maximize your potential development.

1. Hard Worker

You can't change the world by working forty hours a week—not according to Musk, at least. The serial entrepreneur, who routinely puts in eighty hours of work per week, is a noted workaholic who demands the same of his employees. In fact, Musk has made several headlines by suggesting to his employees that they not come to company meetings if they have nothing useful to say and for being hawkish on the job.

In other words, the message is simple: you can't expect big results if you put in minimal effort. Musk summed this up nicely in a public statement, "The idea of lying on a beach as my main thing just sounds like the worst. It sounds horrible to me. I would go bonkers. I would have to be on serious drugs. I'd be super-duper bored. I like high intensity." From this alone, it's easy to see why Musk has achieved such massive levels of success.

This means that we must also take on a mindset of hard work and responsibility if we ever wish to emulate Musk's achievements. Or, to put it another way, we must put elbow grease into our actions so that our dreams can turn into reality.

2. Aim High

One of the incredible traits that Elon Musk has is the fact that he's constantly setting challenging obstacles for himself. Consider for a moment the industries he works in: Space, Clean Energy, and the Internet. The only way he can make a big difference and shake the core of these areas is by taking big risks and defending his ideas to completion. His goal-setting skills are unlike anyone else's, and that's definitely something we can learn.

3. Innovative

How many times have you heard the phrase "Failure is not an option?" As it turns out, the genius entrepreneur lives by a different mantra, one which he's publicly stated, "Failure is an option here. If you're not failing, you're not innovating enough." Sound advice from a man who has completely revolutionized private space travel, created the most energy-efficient vehicles in history and looks to change the face of transportation in the coming years.

Musk is known as perhaps the greatest innovator of our age, a title he wears proudly. Though some critics lambast the serial entrepreneur and scorn his ideas, the reality is that Musk has presided over some of the most successful large-scale tech projects of our age—and none of this would be possible without innovation.

As such, it's time that we began emulating this quality in our own lives so that we can replicate Musk's success and establish ourselves more confidently in the world. With the right amount of innovation, we can help to make the world a more interesting and safer place—but we must take after Musk if we wish to do it.

4. Risk Taker

Musk is certainly no stranger to risks. In fact, it can be said that the serial entrepreneur has built his career of risks, as he has darted from one daring project to another. Simply put, there are few projects riskier than space travel, especially if you are operating as a private institution. Despite this, Musk has turned this unlikely vision into a reality.

The genius engineer has also taken several risks in developing unique energy-efficient technology for his Tesla brand. As part of this, Musk has been behind some of the most important innovations of our time. With no guarantee that these investments would pay off, the serial entrepreneur has embodied the idea of risk taken and served as a blueprint for anyone who wishes to achieve greatness.

Against this backdrop, it's crucial that we begin to understand how Musk operates so that we can also capitalize on risks and achieve a similar level of success. By using Musk as a model, we, too, will be able to align ourselves with greatness and work hard to make a better world manifest.

5. Failure Doesn't Mean "Stop."

If there's something Elon Musk has made clear about himself is that he's motivated to an extremely high degree. The strength of his determination is evidenced by the fact that he decided to keep moving forward with the SpaceX rocket even after several launch failures, and that's only one out of many examples. Failure doesn't stop or deter him, and that's something we can all benefit from learning. The confidence he has in his ideas and what he wants to accomplish is what allows him to make the right choices and eventually hit the mark.

6. Redefine Things

Elon Musk doesn't join an industry; he brings an ax into it and shatters established business models. Tesla Motors is a great example of this; the business model he presented was unlike any other, and he had to overcome many obstacles because of this, but in the end, thanks to his resilience and determination, he managed to redefine an entire industry. Never be afraid of challenging the status quo and bringing something unique to the table; as you can see, the rewards are worth it.

7. Compassion

Those who know Musk know that the Founder, CEO, and Lead Designer of SpaceX, is driven by his desire to help humanity and make the world a better place. In fact, Musk's compassion is in everything he does. From developing energy-efficient electric vehicles that will help save the planet to beginning efforts to make humans an interplanetary species, the serial entrepreneur is always operating with the greater good in mind. This uniqueness places Musk in stark contrast with individuals who are simply out to make a quick buck.

Musk has said as much himself, declaring, "Going from PayPal, I thought: 'Well, what are some of the other problems that are likely to most affect the future of humanity?' Not from the perspective, 'What's the best way to make money?'"

From this, we can gather that what truly spurs the serial entrepreneur forward is compassion for the individuals, for the world, and a desire to truly make the world a better place. If we hope to follow in Musk's footsteps, it's crucial that we cultivate this compassion in ourselves and make it the bedrock of any future plans. In doing so, we'll be able to achieve success like we've never imagined before.

8. Focus

It's simply not possible to revive the electric car industry without focus. It's also not possible to establish the world's leading private space enterprise without being highly committed. In what amounts to an impressive feat, Elon Musk has been able to focus on both these seemingly impossible feats and turn them into reality—all while working on other projects on the side. As a key developer of PayPal, the brain behind SpaceX, the great innovator of Tesla, and the man behind such innovative companies as Neuralink and OpenAI, Musk certainly seems to have his time spread thin. Despite this, the serial entrepreneur has been able to bring unprecedented focus to his work in a way that most people could never dream of.

If you are finding it difficult to focus on one task, it's time to take a moment to learn from Musk. In other words, if the serial entrepreneur can focus on running several of the world's most important enterprises at the same time, it's certainly within the realm of possibility that you can focus on what you need to do so that you can achieve success yourself. This means that one of the keys to following in Musk's footsteps is to generate the same level of focus so that you can make sure that the projects you are working on and the goals you wish to achieve can be successful.

9. Intelligence

It's no secret that intelligence is one of Elon Musk's strongest selling points. While the genius has never publicly released his IQ, it's widespread knowledge that Musk possesses extraordinary critical thinking abilities that have helped him become one of the most successful entrepreneurs of our age. Musk displayed this intelligence from an early age, making the game *Blastar* when he was only twelve years old.

While intelligence is something one is born with and is largely stable over time, there's no reason to think that we can't all better approximate Musk. Rather, those who are looking to follow in the serial entrepreneur's footsteps would be wise to develop their critical thinking skills and to come at life with a more critical eye.

Musk has stated, "(Physics is) a good framework for thinking... Boil things down to their fundamental truths and reason up from there." By following this model, you'll be better able to take after Musk and begin solving the key problems of the world. More importantly, you'll be better able to establish yourself as someone who can move forward with confidence and achieve true success.

10. Humor

Musk is nothing if not funny. The genius entrepreneur has broken traditional molds by routinely appearing on podcasts, shows, and other programs and showcasing his superior wit and humor. In the process, Musk has become one of the most loved cultural figures of our time, developing a near-rabid following. The serial entrepreneur has been able to do this by balancing his intelligence and humor and always staying cutting edge.

This can perhaps best be seen with Musk's appearance on Joe Rogan's podcast in 2018 when he shocked the world by lighting one up. The move, which helped establish Musk as a more personable and likable "celebrity"-type instead of a boring and dry CEO, increased his personal brand and made one fact evident: that humor is crucial to success, particularly when you are building your personal brand.

What this means for us is that we can achieve more success and do better work when we come at things with a bit of humor. Simply put, it's impossible to stay happy long-term if you lack the motivation to see things with a joking eye. Like Musk, we should instead see the world in a brighter way, which will, in turn, help us develop a brighter society for all down the road.

11. Energetic

Musk states, "You have to be pretty driven to make it happen. Otherwise, you will just make yourself miserable." The engineering genius embodies this energy in his own work, whether it's passionately developing new boring techniques to help revolutionize transportation or develop working spacecraft that will reach Mars. In short, Musk believes that energy is one of the most important factors in achieving the goals that you have set.

For the rest of us, it means that we must also be able to generate the same excitement and energy around our own projects if we ever wish to achieve the success that Musk has. Simply put, when you don't come into a project with energy, you aren't going to be able to work at one hundred percent, which causes your work—and ultimately you—to suffer. For this reason, it's crucial that we take this opportunity to learn from Musk that one of the best ways to move forward in life is to do so with a driven energy that can generate success.

12. Business Savvy

By helping establish some of the most successful enterprises of our age, Elon Musk has proven his world-renowned business savvy nature. Simply put, the genius entrepreneur knows how to run a business, and he understands its central concept—branding. In a statement, Musk said, "Brand is just a perception, and perception will match reality over time."

In other words, fake it until you make it. In order to succeed in life and at business, individuals and business owners must know how to establish themselves in the greater context, and this essentially means branding. Whether you are attempting to establish a personal brand (much like Musk has done over the last several years) or wish to establish a strong brand for your business (which Musk has also done), you'll find yourself much more successful when your brand is strong and thriving.

Musk displays his business savvy nature in another way, stating, "Great companies are built on great products." At his core, Musk understands that the best way to establish a brand and connect with consumers is to make a product that's high quality. This is readily evident in the genius's Tesla cars, which redefine the electric car game with every new model.

For those who are wishing to make it in the world of business, there's simply no one better to look up to than Musk. With several of the world's biggest companies to his name, the engineering genius is the ideal role model for anyone looking to achieve high levels of success.

13. Curiosity

According to Musk, "[As a child] I would just question things." This curiosity has followed the genius entrepreneur throughout his life and led to the creation of some of the world's most important enterprises. With PayPal, Tesla, SpaceX, and companies such as Neuralink and the Boring Company under his belt, it's safe to say that Musk has asked plenty of questions—and delivered on countless answers.

One of the key takeaways from Musk's career is that one must always view life critically. By coming at situations with a skeptic's eye, individuals can form important questions about the world around them and, in the process of answering them, deliver a better world for all. This is precisely what Musk is doing, as the serial entrepreneur, who isn't afraid to ask why interplanetary colonization can't be possible, is currently paving the way for private space missions.

In other words, it's time to forget everything you've heard about "curiosity killing the cat." Instead, it's better to follow Musk (and against the grain) and begin to question everything around you instead of simply accepting things as they are. By cultivating this habit, you'll be one step closer to a more productive life.

14. Confidence

How confident is Musk? Setting aside for a moment that this is the man who left a Stanford PhD program to achieve his dreams, the serial entrepreneur has also embarked on daring missions, such as reaching other planets by 2024 and revolutionizing human transportation within the next decade. Musk sums this confidence up nicely in a single quotation, "It's okay to have your eggs in one basket as long as you control what happens to that basket."

This breaks sharply from the mantra of others, who think that putting everything on the line is simply a recipe for failure. Instead, Musk shows that the proper way to move forward and to lead is to have confidence in your plans and in your ability to make them manifest. With the right amount of confidence, individuals will be able to see to it that what they are envisioning can become true.

By taking this page out of Musk's playbook, we'll be able to better orient our lives and move forward in a way that brings us success. As such, it's crucial that we harvest this key trait that Musk exemplifies better than anyone else.

15. Combativeness

When it comes to standing up for what he believes in, Musk has consistently demonstrated a combativeness that is admirable. This can perhaps be best seen in his war with the short-sellers, in which Musk has faced multiple lawsuits and yet refuses to back down from his beliefs that these individuals are damaging his company and doing a disservice to the people. No doubt, this combativeness has played a large part in Musk's extreme success, as the serial entrepreneur has been able to fight for what he thinks is right and bring his ideas to life.

In regard to short-sellers, Musk has famously tweeted, "What they do should be illegal." In doing so, the genius has made himself the face of a new finance movement and become the unapologetic champion for businesses and consumers everywhere. In doing so, Musk has earned himself more fans and an improved reputation.

All this is to say: in order to be successful in life, you'll need to manifest a certain level of disagreeableness. By doing so, you'll be able to take your projects to the next level and be more successful in your life and business.

16. Passionate

It goes without saying that Musk brings an unprecedented amount of passion to his projects. At his core, Musk differentiates himself from other billionaires by putting his focus, not on the money to be made from his endeavors but rather on what his ideas can do for the world. This helps Musk fuel his passion for his work—which, in turn, has led to his extraordinary success.

Musk has gone on record stating, "People should pursue what they're passionate about. That will make them happier than pretty much anything else." From this advice, it's clear that the best way to be successful is to be passionate, as passion can be the driver for several other traits for success.

For this reason, those who wish to follow in Musk's footsteps should harvest their passion and train it at their goals. In doing so, they'll be able to imitate Musk's model and be more successful than they ever thought possible.

17. Visionary

In Musk's own words, "If you go back a few hundred years, what we take for granted today would seem like magic—being able to talk to people over long distances, to transmit images, flying, accessing vast amounts of data like an oracle. These are all things that would've been considered magic a few hundred years go."

This statement highlights Musk's visionary statement and shows his willingness to think ahead. In other words, it doesn't matter to Musk that others may call some of his ideas outlandish and difficult to achieve. Instead, the genius entrepreneur continues to think of pathways to make them achievable, just as the great inventors before him did. This positions Musk in a long line of scientists who have done everything in their power to make sure that their visions become a reality.

For the rest of us, this means that we should also cultivate a better vision of the future and strive to make it come true. In doing so, we'll be able to achieve more success and bring a brighter outlook to the world around us—just as Musk is doing now.

18. Strong Work Ethic

Musk's success also proves that individuals must come into their work with a strong work ethic. In a statement, Musk said, "If you're co-founder or CEO, you have to do all kinds of tasks you might not want to do…. If you don't do your chores, the company won't succeed… No task is too menial."

While the quotation was geared specifically toward business owners, it can be more broadly applied to anyone who wishes to succeed in life. If Musk, who is the genius CEO of several of the world's most important companies, has no problem doing "the chores," neither should you believe that any task is below you. In doing so, you will be able to keep a closer watch on your operations and better gear yourself toward success.

Musk also displays a superior work ethic in his approach to work, which can only be described as passionate and forward-thinking. For those who wish to follow in the genius engineer's footsteps, this means coming into every task with an open mind and doing the utmost to make sure that you succeed.

19. Critical of Self

Though Musk has the reputation of being "overconfident," those who know the genius entrepreneur know that Musk is always thinking of ways to better himself so that he can continue to better the world. In other words, Musk isn't afraid of a bit of self-criticism.

This trait has helped him move on from negative experiences like the one he faced at the end of his tenure at X.com and move into more successful roles down the road.

Of course, Musk knows the limits of this self-criticism. The serial entrepreneur stops short of ridiculing his ideas, even if he has been known to redraw his timetable and admit that his goals were a bit too ambitious within a certain time frame. This shows that Musk strikes the perfect balance between self-criticism and self-confidence. In order to achieve similar levels of success ourselves, we must also find this balance in our own lives so that we can move forward with confidence without losing our check on reality.

20. Obsessive

Want to know the best way to turn your plans into action and your actions into results? If so, it's time to take Musk's model as an example. The serial entrepreneur is known to obsess over his work and his ideas. Where others would simply let far-fetched or seemingly-impossible plans sit on the back burner, Musk strives to make even the most outlandish goal turn into a reality.

This can best be seen with his Hyperloop project. The project would see humans move at the speed of sound through vacuum-tube trains that could be positioned throughout the country. Though the Hyperloop seems like something out of a science-fiction novel, Musk has done his part to make the system a reality, holding two international Hyperloop competitions that have resulted in powerful prototype options.

By examining this model, one fact becomes clear: dreams cannot be made into reality unless individuals obsess over them and get them just right. In other words, if you wish to be successful, the first thing you should do is make sure that you are concentrated on your goals and know how to make them manifest.

21. Free Thinker

For most people, intergalactic space travel seems like an idea cooked up in a cheap science fiction novel, but don't tell that to Musk. The eccentric serial entrepreneur plans on reaching the red planet in a little under a decade, with hopes of colonization and future intergalactic travel.

Sound big? That's because it is. Unlike his contemporaries, Musk is unafraid to think big and go against the grain. Simply put, Musk doesn't dismiss ideas or plans simply because others think that they are impossible. Instead, he chooses to think his own way—and the results have paid off. Musk has succeeded in overseeing the most successful private space enterprise in American history. In the process, his company SpaceX has been able to reach the International Space Station (ISS) on multiple occasions, with trips to the moon and other galactic locations on the horizon.

The lesson is simple: don't be afraid to think outside the box. Sometimes the biggest successes come for those who dare to be different. This means that you shouldn't let others contain your thoughts or keep them in a box. Instead, you should explore your hypotheses and the world around you. In the process, you'll more closely follow in Musk's footsteps and be closer to achieving monumental success of your own.

22. Persistence

It took over a decade for Musk's SpaceX to become the leading private space enterprise in the world. It similarly took years before his Tesla company became the number one electric auto manufacturer in history. This shows that Musk is not afraid to spend time nurturing projects he believes in. Instead, the serial entrepreneur is the model of persistence, standing behind his ideas and doing the most to ensure that his visions manifest in reality.

This means that, in order to be as successful as Musk, we too must move forward with persistence and not simply stop a project because we face adversity. Neither should we give up entirely simply because we encounter setbacks. Musk himself hit a major bump in the road when he was removed from his position as CEO of X.com, a service that would eventually be sold for over a billion dollars to eBay and transform into the world-renowned PayPal. Instead of harboring ill will at this setback, Musk simply shrugged it off, moving on to work on such companies as Tesla and SpaceX, where the genius has established himself as one of the most dominant tech giants and cultural figures of our age.

23. Decisive

Musk stated, "I think it's possible for ordinary people to choose to be extraordinary." The quotation symbolizes Musk's belief in the fact that human destiny is determined by our choices. In other words, in order for us to be successful and follow in the serial entrepreneur's footsteps, we must be firm in our ability to make critical decisions and to stay behind those decisions to make sure that they become a reality.

The serial entrepreneur certainly shows this trait himself. Despite the criticism that Musk is too "irresponsible" on Twitter, he has chosen that route to strengthen his brand. The best part? It's working. Despite the fact that Musk has been involved in a few lawsuits, the Elon Musk hype train is stronger than ever, and more people are buying Tesla than at any time in the company's history.

What does this mean, then? Simply put, it means that in order to be as great as Elon Musk, we need to stick to our guns and not be afraid to make important decisions. In this way, we'll be able to replicate Musk's success in our own lives and do more good for the world.

24. Conscientious

Musk's conscientiousness has played a dominant role in positioning him as one of the most important cultural figures of our time. Orderly, routine, and always on the job, Musk knows what it takes to make his ideas into reality. As part of this, he routinely pulls eighty to one-hundred-hour work weeks and follows a particular model that allows him to focus on his work and bring about real results.

For those wishing to be more successful, this means that conscientiousness is one of the most important personality traits to harvest. While some may be naturally opposed to order and a more thorough work ethic, an examination of Musk and his time at companies such as Tesla and SpaceX can serve as a useful model to growing both personally and professionally. In this way, individuals can begin to establish their own successes and grow in their achievements.

25. Outgoing

Though some fans characterize Musk as a natural introvert, the serial entrepreneur has been able to strengthen his brand based off a natural ability to communicate with his fans and consumers. Despite being bullied as a child in South Africa, Musk has developed into a passionate speaker with the ability to unite audiences around a common goal.

In this way, Musk has tapped into a natural extraversion that has allowed him to get his business message and outlandish ideas to the masses. The results have been nothing short of spectacular. Over the last decade, Musk has watched two of his companies come to dominate their respective fields and has helped launch a cultural shift toward clean and affordable energy.

For this reason, those who wish to be like Musk should harvest their own natural extraversion to better build relationships with individuals, grow their networks, and expand on their business and professional goals.

26. Adaptable

Musk has been able to engineer a successful career on the back of an extremely high level of adaptability that has helped him navigate changes in the business landscape and take his companies to new heights. Despite fluctuations in the market and in consumer perceptions, Musk has been able to keep his companies relevant and on top of tech innovation.

This can be seen in Musk's ability to absorb SolarCity when the company was reaching its final legs and turning it into a useful arm of his Tesla brand. In this way, Musk was able to save the company—which had formerly been run by his cousins—preserve the plight of solar energy across the United States, and make his goal of establishing Tesla as a completely energy-efficient company more feasible.

By following Musk's example, individuals can harness their own adaptability and become more prepared to face the challenges of life—improving their probability for success.

27. Opinionated

One thing's for sure: Musk isn't afraid to speak his mind—or change it. Those who work for the brilliant entrepreneur attest to Musk's tendency to get deeply involved in projects, often requesting several changes. While this makes Musk often difficult to work for, it's clear that his ability to see the bigger picture has helped him become one of the most important men of our age.

In describing Musk, one former SpaceX employee stated that the serial entrepreneur had been known to completely scrap projects that engineers and employees spent nearly a year perfecting. This has established Musk as a strongly opinionated leader who's not afraid to make drastic changes in the running of his organizations.

Individuals who wish to be as successful as Musk must also be able to make such decisions. What's more, they must also be able to speak their minds and be confident in their ability to think critically and make the best decisions given a certain situation. In this way, they'll be able to emulate Musk and achieve greater success in their own lives.

28. Unpredictable

Musk's unpredictability has become the stuff of legend. Simply put, the serial entrepreneur has built an iconic reputation on the fact that no one knows what he will do or say next. This can be seen in his Twitter rants and in his dealing with his enemies, such as short-sellers.

It can also be seen in the numerous quotable statements that Musk has made. On one occasion, Musk remarked, "So next I went to Russia three times, in late 2001 and 2002, to see if I could negotiate the purchase of two ICBMs. Without the nukes, obviously." Musk's purpose for attempting to buy these high-powered Russian missiles? Going to space.

Through this unpredictability, Musk has been able to grow his brand and establish himself as an interesting cultural character. He's also been able to raise his stock value and make life harder for short sellers and others who never know his next move. Those who wish to be successful, then, would do to follow Musk's example so that it's more difficult for individuals to predict their moves (particularly in business) and so that they can build a stronger brand.

The Bottom Line

Elon Musk has established himself as one of the most successful—and most important—individuals of our age. Through companies such as Tesla and the game-changing SpaceX, Musk has been able to redefine technological innovation and win over a generation.

Still, this type of success hasn't come easily. Rather, Musk has built on and cultivated a wide toolset of personality traits that have helped guide him through his personal and professional achievements. By following Musk's example and harvesting these traits, we can also position ourselves as Musk-like figures (muskmelons) on the road to greater success.

In this guide, we covered twenty-eight of the most important traits that have helped Elon Musk become who he is today. By cultivating these traits, individuals can follow in Musk's footsteps and achieve more than they ever thought possible. We can all make our dreams a reality; all it takes is the will to do so!

Elon Musk's Daily Schedule

Elon Musk is a genius entrepreneur who is juggling many things at once. So, of course, he has a packed schedule that he needs to manage. How does he do that? Let's explore.

Firstly, Elon Musk does not have a minute to waste. He needs to utilize every second productively because that is what his work requires of him. However, he also needs to juggle personal and other responsibilities that he has.

Time management is a big aspect of his daily routine. Billionaires don't have the luxury to waste time, so they need to manage every second to the dot. In an interview with a tech magazine, Elon Musk said that he gets six hours of sleep and wakes up at 7 am every day.

According to this, we can come to an understanding that Elon Musk goes to bed around midnight. Once he wakes up, he doesn't eat breakfast so that he can get out of bed, take a shower, spend 30 minutes responding to urgent emails, and then start the day.

If emails require urgent meetings or anything else, he will make changes to his diary for the day. So, the emails of the day determine how his day is going to shape up. However, one thing he doesn't miss is dropping his kids off at school. He does that every day.

After that, he drives to work. He spends almost 80% of his time in the office coming up with new designs for SpaceX and Tesla. If you think 40 hours a week is too much, you will be surprised to hear that this tech genius spends 85 to 100 hours a week working.

He divides his plans into five-minute slots, and each slot is given a specific aim. Doing this aids him in covering more areas within a day. He spends Mondays, Fridays, and some Saturdays at SpaceX. The rest of the days are spent at Tesla.

Even with such a busy schedule, the tech genius finds time for his philanthropy to visit his non-profit organization OpenAI. He only spends five minutes on lunch in a day, and most of the time, this happens during meetings.

After being at work all day, he has an hour or two to spare for other things. He spends this time going to work, dinners, working out at the gym for an hour (he does this only two times a week), and then he comes home and reads books before finally sleeping.

The weekend is free time for Elon, even though he spends a part of his Saturday at SpaceX. However, Sundays are free. He spends this time with his children so he can catch up with them. His favorite thing to do is play video games with his sons on the weekend.

With such a busy schedule, we are amazed at how efficiently he utilizes his time, and if you want to be a billionaire, you can learn something from him.

CHAPTER THREE

BUILDING A SUCCESSFUL 21ST CENTURY BUSINESS - THE ELON MUSK METHOD

Technology has completely revolutionized the business world. People like Jeff Bezos, Steve Jobs, and even Bill Gates all rose to prominence due to the success of their brilliant and innovative technological ideas. The 21st century saw rapid advancements in technology, and with that, many new names entered the business arena, including Elon Musk.

There is no doubt that Elon Musk is one of the most successful people in the world, and he has the net worth to show that. However, this begs the question, how did Elon Musk become the real world's Tony Stark in such a short time? Was it luck? Good decisions? Intelligence? Or all things combined? The biggest assets that Elon Musk possesses are his personality, his skills, and his principles. Mr. Musk is the epitome of a 21st-century success story. He is an inspiration for young and bright entrepreneurs of the 21st century who believe nothing is impossible. If you want to be successful in the 21st century, you need to follow the same steps and principles that Elon Musk follows. Of course, you need to have the same sense of passion, determination, and love for success as described in the previous chapter, but you also need to follow the principles Elon Musk did in order to be successful.

Let's take a look at those principles.

Business Success Principles for the New Age Businesses - The Elon Musk Method

1. Your Business Idea Should be Environmentally Friendly

The 21st century is all about environmentally-friendly businesses. Even companies that have been in business for over a hundred years are turning green. People have realized that if we want a healthy future for the human race, then it is imperative that we start investing in environment-friendly resources. Businesses that are still avoiding environmentally friendly practices are only creating a bad image for themselves in the eyes of the customers. This planet is our home, and it is up to us to protect it. Business personalities like Elon Musk understand this fact. No matter how much he talks about starting a colony on Mars, Earth is still our home, and we shouldn't forget it while racing to reach another planet. Many people criticize Elon Musk for talking about starting a colony on Mars, but no one talks about his efforts to make this Earth a better place. This also shows that if you are doing something right, there will always be people who criticize you, but you have to keep on doing what you are doing. You can also take an example from Elon Musk. SpaceX is not just known for using recyclable parts in their rockets, but it is also known for complete reusable rockets as well. Using recycled material to create rocket parts significantly reduced SpaceX's cost of building new rockets. So, using green and environment-friendly items isn't just going to lower costs for your business, but it will also be beneficial for the environment.

2. Do It for the People and Not for Money

It is commonly believed that businesses are started to earn profits. These days, businesses are much more than just a money-making setup. Some people tend to start businesses because they don't want to work 9 to 5 jobs for someone else and others start their businesses to do good for the general public. Elon Musk is the latter one. Elon Musk firmly believes that once you start working for the betterment of humanity, money eventually follows. You might not see the profits right away, but in the long run, it will be beneficial for you. You have to create an organizational culture where employees are more focused and motivated by what they are doing for the world rather than their paychecks. From start to finish, your product and business practices should all be about doing good for humanity. Ventures like PayPal,

Tesla, SpaceX, and other Elon Musk businesses have all contributed greatly to supporting the general public. Without PayPal, we would have a very big financial mechanism gap; without Tesla, we wouldn't have a trend of environment-friendly cars, and without SpaceX, we wouldn't be thinking about going on a tour to outer space. Even starting a colony on Mars is for the greater good of humanity. In case our home planet is struck with a calamity, the Mars colony will provide us a new place to stay. So, once you shape your products and your entire business to do good for humanity rather than focus on money, you will not only be successful financially, but you will also be loved by the people.

3. Launch the Best Product Possible

Elon Musk took this principle out of another tech visionary's playbook, and that person is Steve Jobs. Like Steve Jobs, Elon Musk also believes that when you want to launch a product in the market, ensure that it is the best version of the product out there. If someone else is doing better than you, then you will be demolished by tough competition in a matter of months. There are many other companies out there that offer electricity-powered vehicles, but why is Tesla so popular all over the globe? It is because the company has launched one of the best products in the industry. It was Elon Musk's vision to have all the advanced technology, including artificial intelligence, installed in Tesla cars.

The best product is a combination of advanced software (including artificial intelligence wherever useful) and exceptionally amazing hardware. So, the technology installed in the car is as equally important as the comfortable seats you place in the cars. The product you offer should be an entire package; otherwise, you will just be leaving room for your competitors to bounce at the opportunity of offering the feature that you did not include in your product. There are very few companies in the market offering high-quality products with a range of amazing features like the companies under Elon Musk. You need to have a proper vision of your product. You need to brainstorm ideas about how you can turn your ideas into the best product(s) the world has ever seen. Look at all sides, study all aspects, and with a keen eye, proper homework, and your natural creativity, you will be able to introduce an amazing product that people will love to buy.

4. Innovation and Creativity: Innovation Should be Fast-Paced

What is the most important asset a company has? Well, the answer is simple. The most important asset a company has are its employees, i.e., the human resource. In order to stay on top, you need to regularly come up with innovative products and strategies, which is not possible without the right type of people. This is why a company's human capital is its most important asset. The employees are responsible for innovations and creativity. Even if the person at the top introduces an idea, the idea has to be implemented with the help of other people in the company.

Being innovative isn't enough; you need to be perpetually innovative. In order to be successful, you need to come up with innovations on a regular basis. You need to be constantly iterating the product taking into consideration customer feedback and new technological breakthroughs. You can use innovations to create a competitive advantage over your competitors and also ensure that you have the best product in the market. You need the right tools and technology to reach high levels of innovation and creativity; however, these tools are useless if there isn't anyone to use them. This is why you need to hire and retain the best people in the industry. These highly creative people will ensure that the pace of your innovation is more than that of your competitors. Elon Musk tends to bring fast-paced innovation in all ventures he participates in. Take, for example, Tesla. Innovative measures have made Tesla cars one of the safest in the world. Not only that, but these cars have self-driving features and a technologically advanced battery. The same or even higher level of innovations can be seen in SpaceX projects. Before SpaceX's Falcon rockets, no one could think about landing a space rocket back on a platform on Earth for reuse. All of this was made possible with the help of constant innovation and creativity.

5. Speed of Execution is Important

You are as fast as your slowest process. The pace of execution is very important. Elon Musk strongly believes that whatever the process, it should be carried out at the fastest pace possible. This means that he does not like lazy or slow people on his team. This is why Musk fired 7 of his top managers at SpaceX, including the Chief of Starlink Satellite Design and Manufacturing. He wanted the entire project to go faster and as the pace of innovation comes from people, so does the slow pace of execution. Elon Musk doesn't shy away from firing people whom he thinks are acting as bottlenecks and slowing down the process. If you are running a business, then you should also focus on the speed of execution. A proper system should be put in place that ensures all processes are being carried out in the quickest way possible. Even after you have installed the required technology and still the process is slow, then it's time for you to start firing people as well. Never compromise on the speed of execution. Imagine you are launching a new product. Now the process of coming up with the product design and the launch of the product should be very fast-paced. If not, then you risk losing the competitive advantage over your product design. Your product design may leak due to the slow pace, and someone might launch a similar product in the market way before you.

6. Adopt Mass Manufacturing

If there is one thing the world can learn from the Chinese, its mass production of goods. Elon Musk is a big fan of mass manufacturing. Manufacturing one prototype or a few lines of products is easy. The real challenge is how you manage the larger stock. Mass manufacturing has a lot of benefits, but it isn't without its challenges. You need large amounts of resources in order to carry on with a mass manufacturing business strategy. If you want to be successful in the 21st century, then you have to follow Elon Musk's method, and Elon Musk believes that it is imperative for businesses to think about mass manufacturing right from day one. It may need high investment, but it will also reduce the cost and time to manufacture the products. If you are someone who thinks like Elon Musk, then you wouldn't just think about lowering cost at the production level; you would think about lowering cost throughout the supply chain. This is what Elon Musk has done with all of his companies. Whether it is the stage of acquiring raw materials or providing post-purchase services to the customers, Elon Musk has tried to reduce cost at every stage. When you are doing mass manufacturing, make sure you reduce cost and increase the speed of manufacturing by maintaining the quality standards and efficiency of the entire process. Tesla, SpaceX, and all other manufacturing units in Elon Musk's companies proudly mass manufacture most of their products. Tesla uses Giga Presses to build multiple bigger parts in a single piece to simplify its vehicle manufacturing process. Giga Presses have proven to be an amazing addition to the manufacturing process. They are the most powerful die casting machines in the world and can reach a maximum pressure point of 61000 Kilo-newtons. Tesla's European plant in Berlin will be operational in 2021, and the company is employing 8 Giga Presses in this plant for intense mass manufacturing. Some of the products have to go through certain stages before they can be mass-produced, but once they reach that stage, they become part of a super heavy mass manufacturing assembly line. This has proven to be a great factor in Musk's success over the years.

7. Vertical Integration

Gradually try to do everything in-house, including the smallest of the hardware and the software —no outsourcing to third party. With battery manufacturing, Tesla has taken vertical integration to new heights – by getting into lithium mining – the raw material for batteries. Vertical integration can give you full control of your business supply chain. It will also help you reduce your overall cost. With vertical integration, you control all parties on both ends of the business, including the suppliers, the distributors, and even the retail stores. This will give you the opportunity to enjoy upstream and downstream profit margins. In addition to a more coordinated supply chain, you can also reduce transportation costs and get more control over all aspects of your business. You cannot be successful if your suppliers or distributors aren't that passionate about the business. So, you need to control both the upstream and downstream parties of your business so that you can ensure that your product maintains its exceptional reputation in the market.

8. Be the First to Market

Ever heard people use the phrase "I make my own destiny"? Well, this principle is a bit similar to that. You don't have to worry about the demand in the market; all you have to worry about is coming up with a product that is so good and necessary to the world that it automatically generates high demand for itself. This is a common occurrence with the products launched by Elon Musk's companies. Elon Musk is a visionary; he has a very creative mind, which is complemented by the innovative and creative minds of people working for him. This is why most of the innovative products they launch in the market are the first of their kind. You can see this with reusable rockets that SpaceX uses and even electricity powered and self-driving Tesla vehicles. Even the projects being worked on at Neuralink are one of their kind. A product at the level of Neuralink Surgical Robot has yet to be manufactured by any of Neuralink's competitors. You can find similar products, but none of them are at the same level as Neuralink's robot. A first mover is like the early bird who gets all the worms. Being first to the market can help you strengthen your brand's position. It can give you more credibility and help you gain all the profits for yourself in the little time you cover the market all alone until a competitor joins in. It can also help you attract loyal customers who would stay with you even after a hundred competitors have joined the fray.

As a business person in the 21st century, your vision should be to create a market for the product or service rather than creating a product or service that the market needs. Write your own destiny by coming up with innovative ideas and then implementing those ideas in the fastest and the most efficient way possible. Don't shy away just because you don't know how people will take your new product. Believe in yourself and your business, and you will see how quickly it generates demand for your products and services.

9. Invest in Improving the Product Instead of Advertisement

In this day and age of social media marketing, you can find many different ways to advertise your products free of cost. You don't have to spend dollars on advertisements when you can spend the same money trying to improve your product. If you have the best product in the market, people will naturally spread positive word of mouth. The way your product looks matters. Imagine if Tesla cars looked like any other generic car on the road. Advertisement wouldn't have helped them in that case. They would just be one of the hundred brands offering the same type of car. However, with Tesla, the design, features, and the Tesla brand speaks for itself. Even if there are no advertisements for Tesla cars, you would still see people talk about them on social media and other prominent platforms. The feel of the end product and a sexy, eye-catching look is necessary for your product.

In addition to spending money on improving your product, the head of the company should also work on creating his/her own personal brand. The same way as Elon Musk and other geniuses like Bill Gates, Steve Jobs, Mark Zuckerberg, and many others have done. When the person at the top creates his/her own personal brand, then they can use that to promote their company products for free. For example, Elon Musk was seen in a cameo role in Marvel's Iron Man movie. He has also been seen in a very casual way on a radio show, and recently, he danced on the stage at one of Tesla's events in Shanghai. How can we forget his vision of colonizing Mars? All of these things have created a 'cool guy' image of Elon Musk, and he has used this to promote his companies. If you are looking to be successful in the 21st century, then you have to let go of this notion that you have to spend money on advertisement to be successful. In today's world, you can find several powerful and efficient advertisement techniques that can yield you great results by spending little to no amount of money provided you have the best product.

These are the nine principles that Elon Musk followed to reach the level of success he has achieved. You might see a lot of people talk about steps you can take to reach high levels of success. Well, in order to be successful, you don't need steps; you need principles that you follow on a continuous basis till the day you retire or hand over your business to your successor. If you want to be successful, then you have to meticulously and continuously follow these principles. Letting go of any one of them can cost your business. The secret is to never forget these principles even if you reach the level of success you were hoping for. Even Elon Musk still follows these principles, and they have made him one of the most successful people in the world. Following these principles *(alone)* will not guarantee success if you don't have the right attitude, passion, and determination. So, before you start focusing on the principles, make sure your mind and body are ready for it as it will need a lot of creativity and hard work.

How Did Elon Musk & Tesla Emerge Victorious from the Cybertruck Unveil Fiasco?

The unveiling event of Cybertruck by Tesla faced a major accident that was made viral within a few moments through news and videos. Later, Elon explained the reasons behind it through his Twitter handle. At the moment of panic, it was noticed that he managed everything well. What happened was that the lead designer of Tesla, Franz von Holzhausen, threw a metal ball at the armor glass window of Cybertruck as a part of a test to showcase its resistance capacity. However, surprisingly, the glass cracked on stage. Elon seemed to be shocked after seeing this and was captured muttering, "Oh my (beep) God." This happened again in the test with another window.

Now, with the accuracy, quality, and testing that Tesla is identified with, what made the glass crack? If you look at the entire event sequentially, you will notice that before hitting the glass with the metal ball, von Holzhausen had smacked the door of the Cybertruck with a sledgehammer. In this test, the door was okay, with not a single impression left behind. After a successful test on the door, the spectators waited for the 'armor glass' flaunted by Tesla. Unfortunately, this time, they failed. Though the door test performed earlier proved the durability of the door, it had an adverse impact on the glass. As Musk explains, the hit on the door prior to the glass test cracked the base of the glass, which consequently splintered the window. They should have tested the glass first and then the door, he adds.

When the vehicle was tested in the lab before the event, it was perfect. Elon confirms this by sharing a slow-motion video of von Holzhausen carrying out the same test. Unlike in the event, the metal ball showed a bouncing-back effect, with no mark left behind. In the actual event, the impact of the previous actions smashed the glass.

However, apart from the mishap on-stage, people seemed to be interested in other interesting features of the Cybertruck, like its unusual looks, impressive design, etc. Also, the big news about the mishap made the Cybertruck a topic of discussion. Elon kept people engaged, even after the unveiling event, by providing more information about its features, such as solar panels for charging. Taking the opportunity to feed their growing curiosity, he replied to their queries and suggestions. He also discussed the future plans for the Cybertruck, which included making it smaller in size for a long-term benefit. It was clear from the increasing engagement on the internet that many people were interested in buying this vehicle. Soon, Elon announced that Tesla has been getting an enormous response and had already received 200,000 pre-orders for the Cybertruck.

To date, Tesla has never paid for any advertisements for this vehicle. The window breaking in the unveiling event was the only major thing. Elon must be credited for turning a negative event into a positive opportunity and using it for publicity.

SECTION 7
REFERENCES

1. Vance, Ashlee (2015). Elon Musk: Tesla, SpaceX, and the Quest for a Fantastic Future. New York City: Ecco Press. ISBN 978-0062301239.

2. Elon Musk – Wikipedia.
   https://en.wikipedia.org/wiki/Elon_Musk

3. Elon Musk (@elonmusk) · Twitter.
   https://twitter.com/elonmusk

4. Teslarati.
   https://www.teslarati.com/

5. CleanTechnica.
   https://cleantechnica.com/

6. "YouTube Channel - Now You Know."
   https://www.youtube.com/channel/UCMFmrcGuFNu_59L0pHcR0OA

7. "YouTube Channel - HyperChange TV."
   https://www.youtube.com/channel/UC1LAjODfg7dnSSrrPGGPPMw

8. "The World's Billionaires List." Forbes. Retrieved April 28, 2019.
   https://www.forbes.com/billionaires/list/1

9. Tesla Inc.
   https://www.tesla.com/

10. SpaceX.
    https://www.spacex.com/

11. The Boring Company.
    https://www.boringcompany.com/

12. Neuralink.
    https://www.neuralink.com/

13. Neuralink – Wikipedia.
    https://en.wikipedia.org/wiki/Neuralink

Get Your Surprise Gift

Thank you for reading my book. To show my appreciation, I've prepared a special gift for all my readers that will help you master all the success principles of Elon Musk. The gift is in the form of regularly updated and free bonus articles, videos, training courses, and lots more.

Access it by visiting: **https://medmantra.com/mm**

Review Request

Reviews are like gold for authors. If you liked this book, please leave me an honest review on any of the following: Amazon, Barnes & Noble, Apple Books, Google Books, Kobo, and Goodreads, or simply send me your personal feedback. I would be so happy.

Link to review URL: **https://medmantra.com/mm**

Made in the USA
Las Vegas, NV
25 February 2024

86303498R00163